THE LAST MARCHIONESS

A PORTRAIT OF LINDY DUFFERIN

THE LAST MARCHIONESS

A PORTRAIT OF LINDY DUFFERIN

EDITED BY HARRY MOUNT

First published in hardback in Great Britain in 2023
by Venn Press

This paperback edition published 2023

Copyright © Harry Mount and the individual
contributors 2023

Cover image: Lindy Dufferin at Clandeboye, after winning the
UK Premier Pedigree Herd Competition, 2007. She is with John
Robertson (left, standing), Scott Robertson (kneeling) and Mark
Logan (right). The champion cow is Clandeboye Gibson Jingle.
Photograph by Brian Morrison.

Edited, designed and produced by Tandem Publishing
http://tandempublishing.yolasite.com

ISBN: 979-8-8655-7059-2

A CIP catalogue record for this book is available from the
British Library.

In Memoriam Lindy Dufferin, 1941–2020

"I wanted to be a great artist but I did not have what was necessary. But I've helped indirectly by loving beauty and now I have Clandeboye to cherish.

I can make Clandeboye a place of wonderment in the future – that will be a real life's work.

Rather than making my ego bump about, getting ever grander, it will be this place that will be my life's work.

It's Sheridan's legacy – that magic man who used to live by my side right here in this room.

Yes – Sheridan and Clandeboye are my legacy – not what I have done but what I've made possible for others to do." *Lindy Dufferin's diary entry, written in the library at Clandeboye, 2017*

"She had no neutral gear." *Tom Stoppard*

"She laughed. I miss her." *David Hockney*

"The Dufferins came into Ireland, played a large role and then died out – while Clandeboye will go on for ever." *Lindy in her diary, 2018*

"Love is in and out of time"

From 'Helen's Tower' by Tennyson, the poem commissioned by the 1ˢᵗ Marquess of Dufferin and Ava to commemorate his mother, Helen Sheridan. The poem is inscribed in brass in Helen's Tower on the Clandeboye Estate.

CONTENTS

Snapshots of Lindy and Sheridan Dufferin in
Lindy's London study.

Lindy Dufferin's obituary in the *Daily Telegraph*, 27 October 2020

The Marchioness of Dufferin and Ava, who has died aged 79, was a painter, conservationist and business-woman, and chatelaine of Clandeboye, one of Northern Ireland's most bewitching houses.

Painting under her maiden name, Lindy Guinness, she was taught by Duncan Grant, Oskar Kokoschka and Sir William Coldstream. In more than 20 shows, in London, Dublin, Paris and New York, she developed her own extraordinary range of styles, from realist to Cubist to abstract.

During lockdown at Clandeboye this year, she produced an astonishing set of landscapes. She was particularly fond of painting her prize-winning herd of pedigree Jersey and Holstein cows, whose milk produces Clandeboye Estate Yoghurt, on sale in supermarkets across Ulster and Ireland.

Every one of the five million yogurts sold has one of Lindy's paintings reproduced on it. "That's how I came to be the most famous disposable artist in the world," she joked in *The Irish Times*.

Alongside her painting, it was Clandeboye – an elegant, Georgian, Soanean house – and its 2,000 acres, a green lung between Bangor and Belfast, that captivated her quicksilver mind and benefited from her boundless energy.

When her husband, the Marquess of Dufferin and Ava, died in 1988, aged 49, he left her his estate. She set about revitalising it, opening a golf course and the Ava Gallery in Clandeboye's Courtyard, and building up the cow herd with her manager, Mark Logan.

Every year, with the Belfast pianist Barry Douglas, she hosted Camerata Ireland, the All Ireland Chamber Orchestra, as part of the Clandeboye Festival. An environmental group, Conservation Volunteers, set up its first Northern Ireland branch at Clandeboye more than 30 years ago. The group nurtured more than 18 million trees at Clandeboye's walled garden before planting them across Northern Ireland.

The Clandeboye woods now host a forest school where local children are taught about trees and wildlife. A new purpose-built school for the children is being constructed in the woods in Lindy's memory.

By the time of her death, Clandeboye was at its busiest since the great days of her husband's ancestor, the 1st Marquess of Dufferin and Ava (1826–1902), Viceroy of India, Governor General of Canada and British Ambassador to France.

Lindy honoured the 1st Marquess's memory by preserving his unique collection of art, books and historic objects. She commissioned his biography, *The Lost Imperialist*, written by Andrew Gailey, the Eton housemaster who looked after Princes William and Harry.

She also renovated Helen's Tower, the fairy-tale spire overlooking the estate. The 1st Marquess built the tower for his mother, Helen, and asked poets, Kipling and Browning among them, to compose poems in her memory, which were inscribed in the tower's dining room. Tennyson's poem began:

"Helen's Tower, here I stand,
Dominant over sea and land.
Son's love built me, and I hold
Mother's love in letter'd gold."

Alongside her painting and conservation work, Lindy was one of the last great country-house hostesses. Everyone from Prince Charles to Van Morrison descended on Clandeboye, where she combined eclectic guests with a brilliant eye.

Among them was David Hockney, first spotted by Sheridan Dufferin, Lindy's husband, early in the artist's career. Sheridan showed Hockney's pictures at the Kasmin Gallery, New Bond Street, which he founded in 1963 with John Kasmin.

Hockney painted and drew Lindy several times. Among her own subjects was the Rev. Ian Paisley, who she painted in a robe and garish tie, with his familiar cry, "No", painted on it.

"It's in the Ulster Museum, I think – perhaps they are too nervous to show it," Lindy said in her characteristic teasing, comic way.

Despite living in Northern Ireland throughout the Troubles, she sailed serenely on, blind to sectarian divisions, opening Clandeboye to all.

She said: "Many of my English friends were deeply concerned about my security but understood I had total confidence about being both a Guinness and a Dufferin and [was] proud of both these cross-border Irish connections."

Lindy said of being a Guinness, "The Guinness family

is fairly big but we all have the sense of us being from the same team."

Serena Belinda Rosemary Guinness was born on 25 March 1941 at Prestwick, Scotland. Her father, the financier and MP Loel Guinness, was a fighter pilot in the Battle of Britain. At the time of Lindy's birth, he was group captain of a squadron at Prestwick Airport.

"He said the birth should take place at the airport to cheer everyone up," Lindy recalled. "New life in the middle of the war, you know."

Her mother was Lady Isabel Manners, the Duke of Rutland's daughter. Her parents divorced when she was nine, and her father married the famed beauty, Gloria Rubio.

Lindy spent a gilded youth shuttling between Belvoir Castle, the Rutland seat, and Palm Beach, where her father and stepmother spent the winters. There, Truman Capote befriended her. "Oh, he was a famous court jester, he had a brilliant mind," she recalled. "He had a slanting approach to life."

As a little girl, Lindy met the French undersea explorer Jacques Cousteau, whose film *The Silent World* (1956) was backed by her father: "I was sitting on a yacht with my father in Antibes. I heard an odd, gurgling sound in the water, and out came a man with a helmet on his head. My father pulled him on to the boat and they started chatting. I had little baby aqualungs, and later I went down with Cousteau."

Lindy often recalled how melancholy her youth was, among these dazzling connections. Her salvation arrived in 1958 in the shape of the Bloomsbury painter Duncan

Grant. She was 17; Grant was 74. She learnt from him at Charleston, the Bloomsbury epicentre in Sussex, for the following decade.

"I was a dizzy, privileged, slightly lost teenager, who happened to be a guest at Firle Place, staying with the Gage family."

At a Guy Fawkes party there, Lindy spotted Grant drawing the bonfire. She recalled: "He stopped and peered closely at me, a look that I was to get to know so well in the years to come. A gentle, intense observation; a gaze of kindness and curiosity, pleasure and amusement. I stayed for the next hour and, during that time, I became intensely excited and knew that the one thing that I wanted to be was a painter."

Lindy called Grant "the nicest, most lovable creature on legs".

She studied at Byam Shaw School of Art, Chelsea School of Art and the Slade. After her first exhibition in 1971 at the Harvane Gallery, she showed in Belfast, Londonderry and Dublin; Browse & Darby in London became her principal gallery. She showed, too, in New York and Paris and was preparing for an exhibition with Jenna Burlingham at the time of her death.

She led painting trips to Marrakech for clients of John Julius Norwich's travel company, Serenissima. She also helped Mother Teresa with her palliative care hospital in Calcutta.

Lindy's second salvation came in the shape of Sheridan Dufferin, her fourth cousin through their great-grandfather, Edward Guinness, 1st Earl of Iveagh.

Their 1964 wedding at Westminster Abbey drew a

congregation of 2,000, among them Princess Margaret. David Hockney joined the couple on their honeymoon, driving across America in a convertible Cadillac.

For all their glamour, Sheridan and Lindy were gentle souls at heart, free of pomposity. She was happiest planting trees on the estate with Fergus Thompson, the head gardener, or painting her beloved cows.

"I call them 'the ladies'," she said. "Countless champions, the best cows in Ireland. It is a journey I am on. I am searching for the essence – or platonic form – of the cowishness of cows."

For someone who did not have the good fortune to have children, she had a gift for engaging, entertaining and enchanting the young, treating them as people in their own right.

INTRODUCTION

Harry Mount

When I last saw Lindy, my dear, dear godmother, in September 2020, there was no sign at all that she would, so very sadly, die, only forty-nine days later, aged seventy-nine.

I was staying at Clandeboye, her delicately classical house between Bangor and Belfast, as I had every year since I was a teenager thirty years before.

Together in that September, we walked and drove round the 2,000-acre estate for hours on end – her energy and fitness supremely greater than mine, despite her being thirty years older. She summed it up in her diary, a few years earlier, "Mummy spotted it. I'm like a pony that hasn't been broken in – still as wild as I was 77 years ago."

We often ran, too. "Come on, Duckles," she would say, heaving her golf bag over her shoulder and running across a fairway on one of her golf courses to get home in time for lunch.

Something was forever driving her on. In her diary in 2018, Lindy wrote, "This morning, I could do nothing – actually I'm always in that situation but I have an internal motor that is always revving up with hope and expectation!"

How Lindy loved Clandeboye. And how she loved Northern Ireland.

When she wasn't painting the ever-changing landscapes of County Down and her prize-winning cows, she was working out ways for making Clandeboye ever more useful – not for her benefit, but for that of Northern Ireland and the people of Northern Ireland and beyond.

***

Born a Guinness, she married the Marquess of Dufferin and Ava, and so felt an affinity with both the Republic of Ireland and Northern Ireland. She was completely blind to sectarian divisions although she realised that Clandeboye could provide, in its flexible way, a refuge for politicians of all creeds.

Peter Mandelson, Secretary of State for Northern Ireland from 1999 to 2001, says, "I remember my first visit to Clandeboye with Reinaldo [his partner] and two dogs, Bobby and Jack, and my favourite photograph is of the three of them hugging each other on Lindy's lawn."

All Lindy wanted was for Clandeboye to have a strong, vital purpose for as many people as possible.

And so, on that last visit in September 2020, we went and looked at her beloved cows and met her devoted herd-manager Mark Logan. Over the last ten years, those cows have produced over five million Clandeboye Estate Yoghurts, sold across Northern Ireland and the Republic.

We then walked on to the forest school she has set up in recent years in the woods – where hundreds of local children have learnt about trees and wildlife under the canopy of beech and oak trees. They loved showing Lindy their dens in the woods and the art they'd done in the forest school – she loved them back.

We looked at the trees she had recently planted with Fergus Thompson, the head gardener.

We drove across the estate to look at a film set that was being erected in a field below Helen's Tower – the enchanted spire overlooking the estate, built by her late husband's ancestor, the 1st Marquess of Dufferin and Ava, in 1861.

One of the many projects Lindy carried out was the tower's renovation – you can now stay there with the Irish Landmark Trust. Whatever she had, she wanted to share.

Staying at Clandeboye always produced this whirl of activities. Over breakfast, she would chat away and plan the day. If there were other guests, there would be visits to see the cows and lunches at Helen's Tower.

When it was just the two of us, she would go off and paint – and have meetings: sometimes with the Conservation Volunteers, who set up their first branch at Clandeboye over thirty years ago; sometimes with local politicians.

She was always thinking, always trying to come up with new schemes to help Clandeboye and help Clandeboye help the wider world. Then, at lunch and dinner, we would meet again to talk.

***

Ever since I was a shy little boy, I noticed that Lindy

– who sadly had no children with Sheridan, her husband – had an affinity with the young.

I was never shy with her. When I was a nervous 14-year-old, she took me out to lunch in London, at the Caprice, the impossibly glamorous restaurant, just before my confirmation, and got me to order the wine.

It was something I'd never done in my life but she suggested it in such a matter-of-fact way that it seemed entirely normal I would do something so abnormal for me.

A similar thing happened when I was five and went to a children's party at Lindy's house in Holland Villas Road in west London. The grandparents there included the former Queen of Greece, Frederica of Hanover. Lindy treated the Queen with such jocular ease that, for several months afterwards, I thought it was standard practice that the Queen of Greece turned up to all children's parties.

Lindy introduced me to country-house life, even if it could sometimes be terrifying. Once, when I was a teenager, she asked me with some wild, dazzling Guinness cousins in their late 20s.

"Should I bring any smart clothes?" I asked her nervously before leaving London.

"Oh do bring black tie – you never know," Lindy said.

On my first afternoon at tea, I asked her whether I should wear black tie that evening.

"Oh do!"

And so, that evening, I crept gingerly down the backstairs, in my Dad's elderly friend's black tie – far too big for me. I pushed open the door of the library a few inches to see all the dazzling Guinnesses in jeans and linen shirts – it was high summer.

I tried to back away, up the backstairs, but one of the Guinnesses spotted me.

"Oh, you've made an effort!" one of them said in an utterly friendly way that still left me feeling crushed. "Do come in."

I spent the rest of the evening sweating, ever more embarrassed, while the jeunesse dorée grew ever more relaxed.

But that was the exception. How Lindy boosted my confidence – and the confidence of hundreds of others. She did it, too, by being tactile – she would thrust her arm into yours or take your hand even if, normally, like me, you aren't very tactile. It all felt very natural.

Lord Dunleath, her neighbour in Northern Ireland, remembers, "Lindy's ability to engage and converse with anyone and everyone was something that we all should emulate."

When you're a child, you don't really have grown-up friends, but that's what Lindy was to me.

In *Breakfast at Tiffany's* (1958) by Truman Capote (a friend of Lindy's father, Loel Guinness), Holly Golightly says, "Anyone who ever gave you confidence, you owe them a lot."

I noticed her giving people confidence again and again when she had guests at Clandeboye. If there was a shy or awkward soul there, Lindy spotted it in a second and she used all her exceptional, innate powers of empathy to bring them out of themselves and cheer them up.

I once saw an awkward teenager, the son of a friend of hers, coming to lunch at Clandeboye. When he turned up, he was bent and cowed, his head almost entirely obscured by his hoodie.

Lindy sat herself next to him at lunch and drew him out of himself. As we moved on to the main course, he was straightening up, his hoodie pushed a little further back off his nose. By pudding, he had slipped off his hood and was wildly gesturing with carefree abandon. Lindy had injected him with a triple-booster jab of confidence in less than two hours.

She did the same with older people, too. Brian Poots, manager of the Northern Ireland Forest School Association, says, "Lady Dufferin changed my life quite literally. She took me under her wing; introduced me to people I would never have dreamed of meeting. It really was like living in an adventure of Lady Dufferin in Wonderland."

Peter Mandelson was enchanted by her on the first evening they met, at a dinner party.

"When I first met her, she was already becoming deaf – so she told me," he says. "She said it was easier talking to me because I had her better (left) ear. She animated and excited as she asked me one question after another about current politics.

"This meant that the person to her right and the fellow diner to my left were barely spoken to during the dinner. It breached etiquette and politeness but Lindy was in full flow and I was delighted to meet and talk to someone who was so warm and interesting. I rather fell in love with her that evening and hopefully the people beside us did not take too much offence."

***

Her gilded background and title sometimes blinded people to her kindness. But she was completely self-aware and knew exactly the effect of her grandness.

Her friend Rupert Lycett Green recalls going to stay at Clandeboye with her and some fellow golfers.

"We golf bores were discussing what clubs we put in our bags," he says. "Lindy, overhearing us, said brightly, 'I have five clubs.' After a moment, the penny dropped."

She once said, self-mockingly, to a friend of mine, "The awful thing about people like me is you can always look us up somewhere and find out all about us."

In her diary in September 2019, a year before she died, she wrote, "A title does affect people in the strangest way. I'm sure this happens with me but oddly I don't feel it, except that it makes me less deferential than I normally would be. There is a certain unwritten law that all the nobs are a family or tribe and that I have a complete right to be part of it.

"However, I also realise that I was Miss Lindy till I was twenty-four and then I became a marchioness – I was NOT born a marchioness."

Lindy, like most funny, clever people, could work at two levels. She could see the way the world looked at her and also see the way things really were. She could stand back and look at herself with detachment.

As the historian Professor Roy Foster says in this book, "She was such a life force and did a lot of good, while retaining her unique mixture of grandeur and 'divilment'."

It was typical of that divilment that, for all the awful bleakness of her overwhelmingly sad funeral at Clandeboye, Lindy asked for her coffin to be taken to church in the back of the pick-up belonging to Mark Logan, her beloved farm manager.

Instead, it was understood that, for all her wonderful lack of pomposity, it wasn't quite right. She was carried to her eternal rest in a simple willow coffin by horse and cart, decorated with plants from Clandeboye by Fergus Thompson, her adored head gardener.

***

Again and again, people comment on her wildly diverging but strangely complementary characteristics. Professor Sucheta Mahajan of Jawaharlal Nehru University, New Delhi, describes first seeing her at tea in Clandeboye:

"I was taken aback by her appearance. I expected a dowdy English royal-type figure but was introduced to a figure out of the back page of a literary work – carefully casual jeans, tousled hair – who gave us organic yogurt, instead of scones, for tea."

The following year, Professor Mahajan returned to Clandeboye with a Trinity College group during a literary festival. He says, "I saw a totally different side of her: organiser, host, hands-on with everything, including taking little children for a nature walk and telling them stories in a copse in the woods on the vast estate.

She wore her family's lineage and legacy so lightly, tramping around in wellies and khaki jackets, that by the end of my visit I found myself admiring her initiative and generosity."

Gerry Summers, her first head gardener at Clandeboye, remembers how helpful Lindy was when his late wife, Rosemary, was on a waiting list for an operation.

"She was very friendly with my wife," he says. "She had a word with the hospital and my wife got in the next day. She'd say there's no use in having a title if you can't use it. She was a great lady."

Lindy was perfectly happy to play the title game if it helped someone else. But she could also see through it all. Staying with the Marquess of Bute in Scotland in 1973, she wrote in her diary, "I've been feeling a bit miserable. Couldn't quite fit into all the atmospheres – felt liverish and this is always the problem I seem to face once I'm trapped into behaving like a 'lady'!"

You can see why people might be impressed – or bamboozled – by her title. It was quite a handle. I remember finding it very confusing writing thank-you letters for her lovely presents (I still have a much-prized Dunlop Maxply tennis racket; what joy when she took me to *101 Dalmatians* for a tenth birthday treat) as a little boy: the Marchioness of Dufferin and Ava wasn't easy to spell.

After she died, I got a letter from someone who still felt mortified for laying out two invitations at a reception for Lady Dufferin and Lady Ava. Still on her mantelpiece in London when she died was an invitation to Holyroodhouse for a private view of *Four Centuries of Paintings from India*. It was addressed to The Lady

Dufferin and Lindy Hamilton-Temple-Blackwood. How was the person who sent the invitation to know they were the same person?

Lindy was alive to the flattery that comes to someone in her position. In 2019, in her diary in Istanbul – she was at a party held by Ömer Koç, the Turkish businessman and a contributor to this book – she wrote, "Honestly, I've been spoilt to such a point that I almost want to believe I'm all the things people say I am!!"

***

All this explains why Lindy wasn't deferential to anyone. She had complete social confidence.

A few months before she died, at breakfast at Clandeboye she asked me what I'd like to do: "Play golf, go for a swim – or meet Arlene Foster [a contributor to this book, then the First Minister of Northern Ireland]?"

Interested in politics, I went for the third option. Lindy texted the First Minister and it was fixed – Arlene Foster would come to lunch at 1pm that day.

As Lindy and I went out to greet her, she suddenly said, ducking down a side passage off the hall, "Oh, I've got to clean my golf shoes – you meet her."

Off I went, a little nervous, to meet the First Minister. She turned up a few minutes later with her driver and her security detail.

Later, after Arlene Foster left, I said to Lindy, "I must admit I was a little nervous when you went off to clean your golf shoes. Do you ever get nervous, meeting anyone?"

"No!" she said, laughing, with no arrogance – just complete honesty.

In fact – as I found out only after she died when I read her diaries – she wasn't cleaning her golf shoes. She had just discovered some urgent business news at Clandeboye which she had to deal with immediately – but didn't want to spoil the day with serious matters.

***

That confidence didn't mean she was smug or complacent. She often admitted to melancholy, enduring sadness on the death of Sheridan, and a lack of confidence about her education. She once pointed out a little paper message she'd attached to her watch. "Don't worry!" the message said.

Her diary entries are full of strict instructions to herself to cheer up and do good, like this one in 2019:

"Lindy, be thankful

Great, thrilling day ahead

I will paint beautiful images

I will try to love others at all times

I will be generous of spirit."

Later that year, she wrote in her diary, "There is a danger of slumping, which is NOT the way forward."

She was frank to friends about Sheridan's inability to have children. As she confided in her diary in 1973, "I think it has been written that Sheridan and I cannot have children for some long-term reason... If tomorrow I was told that I could have one of his, my joy would know no bounds; my heart and soul would expand, my ability to love treble. The ordeal and future I would face with all the animal force and bravery that must fill a mother's soul."

Later in life, she would often tell me she wouldn't have been a good mother. Not true, I'd say, thinking of her extraordinary ability to show affection, just as a god-mother, let alone as a real mother.

***

That complete social confidence meant she could look at everyone objectively – and warm to the best human qualities that rose above the characteristics of the great and the grand.

I once stood with her at a party at Spencer House. She gazed, rapt, at a line of businessmen literally queueing up to meet Prince Charles, as he then was. "Look – one of them's actually sweating!" she said. "Why are they so scared?"

In fact, she delighted in throwing aside the accoutrements of grandness – literally. In a posthumous tribute to Lindy, the artist Tom Hallifax describes going with her to the west of Ireland on a painting trip: "You stripped down to your pants and dove into a black island lake to steal a waterlily for your garden. On our last trip across the Moroccan Rif Mountains to the blue city of Chefchaouen, you were as comfortable in a tiny hostel as you were in gilded halls – perhaps more so."

Maybe because she hadn't had the happiest of child-hoods in the grandest of families, she could see through gilt veneers. When I once showed her a fawning book about her parents' upper-class generation, she said, "What you must remember is that they were all horrible!"

I often asked her about her extraordinary upbringing – with the likes of Truman Capote ("He was so wicked – I loved him," Lindy said) and Gloria Guinness (her It-Girl stepmother).

How dashing it all seemed. Lindy learnt to fly helicopters in her father's lap but, as she put it, "I sometimes think he was better with machines than he was with women."

She would politely tell me about them all with a touch of world-weariness: not rejoicing in their fame and glamour, but slightly depressed that people should be so interested in these often flawed, spoilt figures. Lindy had known them all so well that she could take them at face value.

At one point in her diary, she wrote, "A classic conversation about trying to sack a secretary/groom – it was how I was brought up with Gloria and Daddy and it was fascinating to see how I still resent it and want to talk about plants, thoughts, ideas etc."

It was a world she was born into but always viewed at one remove. Staying with the Duke of Marlborough (Bert) in 1967, she writes, "I sat next to Bert at dinner. 'Hum… 30 housemaids at 5 shillings a week' was his retort when asked about the servant problem."

Again and again, she saw through, with her X-ray specs, to the chilled bones of rich men's souls. In 1974, Aristotle Onassis told Lindy that he wished he'd kept a diary, like her, "to be able to recall incidents which at a later date would be of use in a lawsuit".

Jackie O, by contrast, Lindy wrote in the same entry, "is as thin and breathless, hypnotic and charming as she should be".

Her life had been laid out for her along these golden tramlines. In fact, when she was 16, she went to a fortune-teller who turned out to be eerily accurate. Lindy recorded in her 1957 diary the fortune-teller's prediction (my comments in capitals):

"I meet my husband when I'm being presented and he is to have a very much larger title than mummy [CORRECT]. But I do not marry until I'm 23 [SPOT ON – IN 1964], never to be regretted.

I dislike to be bossed [CORRECT].

I'm going a long way in the world [CORRECT].

I'm to be a great hostess [CORRECT].

I'm better bred than Herky & Dom Cadbury [UNCERTAIN]."

In her diary for 1957, when she was 16 – the earliest surviving volume in a series she continued all her life – she also presents a picture of a rather bleak, gilded existence.

The opening page has the usual teenager's warning: "This book is very Private! Please do not read it, not even for a joke!!"

But then Lindy plunges into a world lived in by not many other teenagers, then or now. The opening lines of the diary, for 21 August 1957, read:

"Spent a quiet day on board *Calisto* [her father's yacht]. Left Monte Carlo this morning and went to the islands off Cannes."

That September, she went to stay with her mother in Coughton, Warwickshire. There the artist Paul Maze (1887–1979), an Anglo-French painter known as "the Last of the Post-Impressionists", comes to stay. He does a drawing for her of his house in Twyford, which she sticks into her diary, the first of many great artists she and Sheridan would collect over the years.

At an early age, Lindy had an introduction to the great and the good that left her unfazed by fame, not least when she saw its less distinguished representatives.

That September of 1957, staying with her father in London, Lindy writes:

"Randolph Churchill [Winston's son] was staying the night here... It was most embarrassing because Randolph was very drunk and began to insult Bob Young over his railroads so Papa after a time removed him but he insisted on coming back and so we spent an awkward evening."

There were some dazzling high-society moments, too. In October 1957, she was in Paris:

"At 11 o'clock I went to Dior to try a dress by myself... Gloria [Guinness, her stepmother] this morning gave me a beautiful suit which was from Balenciaga."

Later that week, Lindy wrote, "The Dutchess [sic] of Windsor came ... I did a show of Rock & Roll. It was all great fun. Bon Soir!"

There were thrilling incidents, too. The month before, she wrote, "Life has been one long joy. Been kissed by Prince Bourbon, Stavro and endless more!"

But, in the end, the glamour mattered for nothing. When that was stripped away, all that mattered was whether they were good, kind, clever or sympathetic company. She was much more interested in cows than Cowes.

***

Her vision as a painter – honed by studious observation – combined with these characteristics to produce a unique character. More conventional souls sometimes thought her a little crazy. In fact, she was in complete command of herself and how she came across. She just felt beholden to few conventions – and so, unmoored from those ties, she soared above the tribe.

Underneath that grand exterior, a considerable intellect was whirring away. Andrew Gailey, the former Vice-Provost of Eton, who wrote the biography of the 1st Marquess of Dufferin and Ava commissioned by Lindy, said, soon after her death, "I thought that the obits in *The Times* and *Daily Telegraph* didn't capture what was magical about her and instead portrayed her as a rather dotty aristo whose heart was in the right place. She could play the dotty aristo when she wanted to but she was always razor-sharp underneath."

Some people did wrongly think of her as a dotty aristo. What came across to them as dottiness was in fact originality – an unusual mind which remained unfettered by quotidian thought, thanks in part to her privilege and the money that allowed her near-complete freedom of movement and thought.

She might sometimes play up to the dotty marchioness image, as she did in 2008, when Sainsbury's outbid

Tesco to sell organic yoghurt from Clandeboye.

When Lindy was asked by a journalist what market she was targeting, she said, "Haven't a clue, I've never been shopping."

That wasn't *quite* true. But she knew exactly what she was doing – and any criticism of the remark was vastly outweighed by the generous publicity it brought. David Hockney told her, "I don't believe I have ever laughed so much in my life."

She once said to me in Holland Villas Road, at her west London house, "What I'd really like to do is go to the supermarket and buy a pint of milk one day."

I offered to accompany her on this daring mission but she had already moved on to the next joke. The dotty marchioness act was always undercut with jokes, directness and blasts of wit.

She was eccentric but she also knew that turning up the eccentricity dial could be amusing and also, sometimes, an effective facade to keep people at bay. As Lola Armstrong, the Clandeboye archivist for thirty years, puts it, "There was something of the music-hall artist about her. I did lead a varied time at Clandeboye. It was great fun and there was never a dull moment – not least when the muniment room door opened and the voice said, "MRS A! I was thinking of doing…""

Oh, how funny she could be, often combining a modern directness with an old-fashioned manner and grand accent to fine comic effect. She would call a young man "frightfully sexy", knowing how flattered he would be, at the same time realising how amused everyone else in earshot was. After a few beers, she would say, "I'm a little tiddly" – but never in an affected way.

She used eccentric, old-fashioned words in a fully conscious way, to be funny. Fiona King, whose mother Elaine worked for many years as Lindy's much-loved cook at Clandeboye, remembers peeling potatoes in the kitchen there one day as a 16-year-old, helping out her mother.

"It was a funny, wee thing," says Fiona. "I heard the gravel on the ground – it was Lindy. There was a rap at the window – 'Cooeee, cooeee.' And she'd talk and talk and talk – and we have ten guests coming.

"'Are you having fun?' Lindy asked me.

"'Yes, I'm having fun.'

"'What are you making?'

"And so it went on. We had a lot of work to do. She went off for a walk. And then we heard the footsteps again. Elaine and I hid behind the island when we heard the footsteps.

"'Yoo-hoo. Cooeee.'

We were down for quite a while."

Fiona said this with fondness, as she recalled Lindy buying her rainbow-coloured trousers for Christmas. "Lindy loved fun," says Fiona.

***

In her diaries, too, Lindy has a funny, original writing style with a taste for amusing, slightly shocking words. In September 2019, she wrote, "We are cutting off the nipples of life because we are so greedy."

She was keen too on producing a great flood

of words. At one point in her diaries, she wrote, "Darling Sheridan, are you really on that cloud looking down as I write this diary? If so, I love you so much and you are more and more in my whole infrastructure-mind-body-love-passion-actions."

Lynn McConnell, of the Northern Ireland Forest School Association, remembers that "The first time I met her, she was upside down in a headstand when I walked into the room."

That sort of behaviour might have been too self-consciously eccentric in some people; rude in others. Lindy's eccentricity was really originality of thought and physical behaviour (through elaborate hand gestures, she acted out her thoughts to great comic effect), rooted in affection, unbound by fear of convention.

"She was totally unjudgemental – more than most of us I suspect," says her friend, the film director Tristram Powell. "She greeted you as if you were the one person in the world she wanted to see, even if people were swirling round. It was as if the two of you were briefly part of a shared conspiracy. There were plenty of unseen complications in her inner life, I felt, but she made light of them. A strong, brave character."

***

Her unique combination of confidence, unworldly innocence and wit meant she could charm people even when she said accidentally outrageous things.

Lindy's cousin Miranda Payne remembers being at a party with Lindy in the Chelsea Physic Garden.

"We were sitting on a bench with Lindy when the actor Damian Lewis came up to have a chat. Keith [Payne, Miranda's husband] whispered to Lindy, 'He's the actor from *Homeland*.'

"With all her enthusiasm, Lindy said to Damian, 'I know – you are the boy from Homebase, it's my favourite shop!'

"Damian took it well. He was amused. He said, 'I have been called many things but this is a first.'

"Lindy's blue eyes twinkled."

She had incredible force of will. Not many people could persuade the Aga Khan's brother, Prince Amyn Muhammad (whose mother, Joan Yarde-Buller, had been married to Lindy's father, Loel Guinness) to look at their cows. With Lindy, there was no choice.

As Lola Armstrong, the Clandeboye archivist, says, "She was good at using her guests in the best possible way. When Adam Zamoyski, the distinguished historian, came to stay, she immediately got him to give a talk in the Banqueting Hall."

***

When I was using voice recognition to dictate the hand-written chapter by Clandeboye's head gardener Fergus Thompson, the computer kept on turning Lady Dufferin into "Lady Different".

By some magic alchemy, the computer had divined Lindy's spirit. She *was* very different.

When a friend of mine told her that her grandmother counselled against marrying someone "different" – i.e.

outside upper-class circles – Lindy was horrified. "What's wrong with different?" she said.

"It sounds condescending to call her one of the great eccentrics of our time, but she was (that much over-used word) unique," says the writer Richard Davenport-Hines. "She was so vivid, distinctive, generous, difficult; never spoilt or absurd, though sometimes perilously close to being so; fascinating, delightful, and profoundly original. Her life had so many interesting elements: her character was not the least of them. The parties in Holland Villas Road, the rejuvenation of Clandeboye, the private and public charities, her paintings, the sensible dignity of her marriage.

"She gave wonderful lessons in how to live wisely, generously and well."

***

It must be admitted that she could be a force to reckon with, particularly at Clandeboye – which she called her "playpen". And it's true that, sometimes, her froideur with friends over a disagreement could linger for weeks before she kissed and made up.

I once spent a weekend with her at Clandeboye when, halfway through, she decided to stop talking to one of the guests. Neither he nor I ever knew why. Normal relations were resumed a few weeks later.

She could be demanding. Going to Clandeboye, aged 19, I took my girlfriend at the time. She didn't play golf but Lindy and I did. So we played the new golf course at Clandeboye. There weren't any flags yet. So Lindy just said, "Alice, you be the flag."

And so, for several holes, Alice ran ahead and stood over the cup, risking life and limb – more from Lindy's elegant chips than from my muffed efforts.

It all sounds terribly spoilt, I know. One of her former employees once said, "Lady Dufferin's a terrible old slave-driver." But I know Alice didn't mind. There was no malice in Lindy's request. And that former employee was bereft at her funeral.

Lindy maintained a clever balance with the people who worked for her. She was genuinely friendly but also maintained a professional distance.

Her housekeeper in London, Ana Gama, remembers Lindy calling her "Anapots" at jokey, informal moments – and "Ana" when something serious had to be done.

"She always called me Jack-Jack, which I didn't like but didn't want to tell her," says Jackie Shields, her last cook at Clandeboye. She also remembers Lindy crying, "Look at my abs!", and lifting her shirt.

Underneath it all lay a profound generosity of spirit, as well as a material generosity.

Jackie says, "She asked how much a bottle of wine would cost. I said £7–£10. Then she gave me a bottle. My daughter looked it up and it was £37. She gave me champagne for my birthday. She kept my birthday in her diary."

Lindy took well-known guests, like Northern Ireland First Minister Arlene Foster, to meet the staff. When Prince Charles came, she had photos taken of them all and gave two to each of the staff.

It may all sound a little noblesse oblige. But, more

often than not, noblesse does not oblige. Lindy did. She realised her extreme advantages in life and, rather than wanting to keep those advantages to herself, she wanted to share them.

When her friend, the artist Catherine Goodman, the Founding Artistic Director of the Royal Drawing School, had a teaching session at Clandeboye, Lindy asked her cook Jackie Shields's daughter Samantha to join in. Jackie remembers, "Samantha's a great artist – and the artist Martin Mooney took Samantha under her wing.

"She was very thoughtful. Every night I came in, she asked how my two wee dogs were. She'd ask you questions."

***

John Betjeman had been a great friend of Sheridan's father, the 4th Marquess of Dufferin and Ava, killed in the war by a Japanese shell in 1945, aged thirty-five. By a strange coincidence, he died in Burma, extremely close to Ava, the ancient Burmese capital, from where his grandfather took the name of his title.

Betjeman wrote a poem to his friend on his death:

> Friend of my youth, you are dead…
> Humorous, reckless, loyal –
> My kind, heavy-lidded companion.

In his verse autobiography, *Summoned by Bells*, Betjeman

talked about his 1920s weekends at Sezincote House, the Anglo-Indian pile in Gloucestershire, home to his Oxford friend Michael Dugdale:

> First steps in learning how to be a guest,
> First wood-smoke-scented luxury of life
> In the large ambience of a country house.

Lindy taught me how to be a guest, happily introducing me to friends from her generation and lifelong friends from mine.

She also introduced me to the perils of country-house life – notably when she suggested playing a hole on her golf course on the way back to the house, with all the weekend's guests in tow.

A little nervous, I swung the club, a mighty driver, off the tee. And yet the ball didn't move. It still sat on its tee, as I heard a terrible screaming.

Lindy's beloved dog, Ava, also named after the family's title, was on its hind legs, blood pouring from her nose and letting out a keening howl. She had run straight at me as I drove and had caught the three wood straight on her snout.

Lindy rushed towards me, gathered Ava in her arms and raced off to the vet in Belfast. I spent the afternoon, head in hands, in the library, as various guests came shuffling through, each patting me on the back, and saying, 'Bad luck.' One of them later told me he spent the whole weekend thanking the Lord it wasn't him who'd committed this terrible sin.

Ava came back, fully intact, thank God, from the vet.

And Lindy never got angry with me – a week later, she told me, Ava raced in and snatched her ball but missed Lindy's clubhead by an inch.

***

And Lindy didn't mind – well, not always – if someone disagreed with her. I once played tennis with her and my Dad (Ferdinand Mount, who writes elsewhere in this book) at Clandeboye. We needed a fourth. My mother, a reluctant but good player, agreed to play but only if no one told her off.

A few points in, Lindy said to my mother, who was about to serve, "Duckles, you really shouldn't leave balls by your feet." Mum silently put down her racket and walked off court. Lindy said nothing.

She had rarely been told off in her life but she accepted the disagreement of those she respected and loved – particularly her adored husband, Sheridan, the most unaggressive of souls.

One day, she was discussing the idea of building a Burmese bridge over the stream leading down to Clandeboye lake.

Sheridan, reading the papers, looked up and said, utterly gently, "This is an Irish estate. There can't be a Burmese bridge."

Lindy said nothing more. She wasn't angry; she just realised he was right.

She could be very outspoken, though. Arriving in Venice, a great friend suggested they go to the Cipriani, the smartest hotel in town, then owned by her Guinness cousins. Sitting down to dinner outside on the terrace, she declared, far too loudly, of her fellow diners, "These are the horrible sort of people I grew up with."

More often than not, the directness was delivered with funny top-spin. When I last saw her at Clandeboye in 2020, she said, prodding my paunch, "I've still got a good body, and a smaller tummy than you!"

Aged 79, she proceeded to do a series of gravity-defying stretches on the floor of the dining room to comic effect. If you look at pictures of her, someone is usually laughing in the background.

Even when she was being demanding, though, it was rarely for her own benefit. The painter John Craxton (a friend of Lindy's) "enjoyed himself by sharing enjoy-ment" said his biographer, Ian Collins – and the same went for Lindy.

In her desire to keep the Clandeboye show on the road – and to keep the merry-go-round turning – she would do anything for her friends and staff; but also ask a lot of them.

In 2005, when we were about to have lunch at Helen's Tower, that fairyland turret up in the woods above Clandeboye, I mentioned that Arsenal, the team I support, were playing in the Cup Final that afternoon. Walter Corr, who looks after the Tower, was despatched all the way back to Clandeboye to fetch a telly and lug it all the way up the steep staircase. My protests about this monstrous proposal meant nothing – and I got to watch Arsenal beat Manchester United on penalties.

***

Lindy was a consummate host but was also very happy on her own. She was an introvert-extrovert: extremely adept in company, but delighted to escape from it all.

After another rushed-off-your-feet weekend at Clandeboye, she'd say, "I'm afraid that's the last time I'm doing one of those." Several months later, the phone would ring: "Pupples, are you free in the second weekend of June?"

In her diary in August 2019, she wrote about this paradox: "I feel sad this morning. I'd love to have a true companion. I want to be alone and at the same time I want companionship. I have to accept moments of loneliness as part and parcel of having my freedom."

That Christmas, she wrote in her diary, "I feel very lonely!! Christmas – without doubt, it is the one time I find so difficult not to have a family to love and to be with; and for some reason I find it impossible to set something up. I don't dare do a Clandeboye Christmas because I need someone to do it with."

***

In one of her obituaries, the *Daily Mail* made a sublime typo: they called her a "conversationist" rather than a conservationist.

In fact, they were right: she was a conversationalist like nobody else (as well as a great conservationist). She was extremely funny: a brilliantly skilled tease who could diagnose exactly what you thought and what you were like and, in an affectionate way, joke about your characteristics. I roared with laughter so often with her.

But, still, she took her duties extremely seriously – even if, at the same time, she could joke about them and observe their funny aspects. She spent many evenings discussing the future of Clandeboye after her death. She was the last of the Dufferins – well, to be precise, she was the last Marchioness of Dufferin and Ava. The marquessate died out with Sheridan's death in 1988. His cousin Francis Blackwood became Baron Dufferin and Clandeboye, succeeded by his son John Blackwood as the 11th Baron in 1991. But there are no male Dufferins now in a direct line from the 1st Marquess.

Lindy never showed off about the history of Clandeboye, the Dufferins or the important objects the family had gathered over the centuries. In fact, she knew that history inside out, despite being a questing modernist in her art.

She painted in ever more avant-garde styles, constantly experimenting. Tom Stoppard says, "I caught her at the best moment in her Cubist cow movement before she took it too far!"

Of that movement, Lindy said, "I am searching for the essence – or platonic form – of the cowishness of cows. They intrigue me."

Peter Mandelson loved the cow pictures: "I bought some paintings by Lindy but, to my eternal regret, I did not buy any paintings of her famous cows (no money). I last saw her when I bought some more pictures in her show in Cork Street."

Lindy acknowledged in her diary that she'd been taught by so many greats – from Duncan Grant to Kokoschka – that she had to fight to track down her own style:

"I might have found my own voice – a sort of mixture of me and so many masters that I have studied and loved... How to use colour instead of line – that seems to be my quest at the moment.

"I am an artist because it is a necessity. It is the way I can let out – express – what I feel about being alive." – Diary, 2019.

With her energy and curiosity, she went through many different painting styles. In her early works, you can see a strong Bloomsbury influence in her landscapes and still lifes.

But she was always keen to start anew. She experimented with Impressionism in her pictures of the Clandeboye interiors, particularly the library. In recent years, she had reached an almost abstract level in her County Down landscapes.

During lockdown, which she spent at Clandeboye, she produced over 100 canvases in preparation for a show.

Her cook at Clandeboye, Jackie Shields, remembers Lindy saying to her, "I love this lockdown. I shouldn't be saying this. I don't want to go to London to all those posh dos." Jackie says, "She loved it – she was king of the castle."

Lindy said so in her diary in 2020: "It has been this enforced but magical stay."

It is some consolation in the grief over her death that she spent lockdown so happily at Clandeboye. Shortly before she became ill, the pandemic restrictions were lifted and she could have gone back to London if she wanted. But she kept putting off her flight – she was content at Clandeboye.

As she wrote in her diary at the end of 2019, just before the pandemic, "I have an overwhelming feeling that I would rather be here than anywhere in all the world. Clandeboye is a paradise on earth."

And she painted furiously in lockdown, boosted in her efforts by putting her pictures online. In her diary in March 2018, she wrote, "I have to admit having an audience for my work, paintings, makes a huge difference. Now I paint every day and if I am reasonably pleased and put the painting on Instagram and I then get 160 or even 200 people saying they like it – also I get messages and feel I have an audience. This NEVER happened before. In fact, I had no reaction; just painted in a vacuum – now I'm no longer in that situation and it thrills me."

Her pictures particularly suited Instagram. The poet Sean Borodale saw them online and admired them as "wet gemstones on fire", borrowing roughly from Nick Serota's description of Howard Hodgkin's paintings.

She wasn't averse to putting pictures of herself on Instagram, too. As Daryl Hendley Rooney, a graduate student at Trinity College Dublin who came to a Clandeboye reading party, wrote, "In her last post on Instagram, Lindy provided a picture of herself sitting in the digger bucket that had cut the first sod on the site where the Clandeboye Yogurt factory was being built. She finished the post with 'Nothing ventured, nothing gained!!!!'"

She retained a happy optimism even in her final illness. In her last weeks in hospital, she wrote, "I'm

contemplating writing a book called 'From 80 to 90'."
Sadly it wasn't to be.

Although she was searching for the Platonic nature of
things in her painting, like all artists she acknowledged
that it was important for other people to like your work.
I remember her delight at selling pictures at a Paris
show to people who didn't know her personally.

Success in painting gave her extreme pleasure. Here
she is, writing in her diary in 2019:

"At long last, I almost have a job and that is being an
artist. I made 75,000 last year in sales and this was after
giving 40 per cent to the dealers.

"Thank you, O Lord, for making this possible. I have
to paint – it is really becoming a job for me, which is
so, so important for me in my old age – to paint till I
die – to become the harbinger of kindness and giving
and seeing beauty. This should be my quest – I've the
money, space, privilege to do this. I will really try. Praise
be to God."

She and Sheridan collected modern pictures, and
spotted modern artists, with a rare eye. But they both
deeply appreciated the hallowed status of history and
the past. They added to and conserved their historical
collections and knew and understood their significance.

Soon after their 1964 marriage, Sheridan and Lindy
redid all the curtains and covers at Clandeboye, using
6,000 yards of material. They bought 18th-century Irish
furniture and glass. Lindy created the extraordinary
Duncan Grant room, filled with her collection of his
paintings. They rehoused and added to the Indian
sculpture collection. They modernised the heating and

moved the kitchen next to the dining room from a remote wing, where Lindy then set up her studio.

And they built the grand stone steps in front of the house. In a typical combination of acute observations, Lindy modelled them on steps she'd seen while drawing at the Royal Hospital Chelsea. And, ever on the lookout for a good deal, Lindy heard the old platform at Strabane Station was being demolished – the stone was promptly used for the steps.

In the Clandeboye guidebook, Lindy wrote, "Over the years, we have presumed on our talented friends, using their skills in rearranging the collection of books, picking out gold lettering, designing trompe l'oeil devices and rehanging the paintings. On one of these occasions, David Hockney made an etching of the window and chair in the library [see plate section]."

It all added up to quite a heady combination. As Lindy wrote in the guidebook, "It is a house of dreams and enchantment that fill my thoughts and, as I grow older, the pleasure of being part of it grows greater."

Thanks to Lindy – and Sheridan – Clandeboye remains the extraordinarily crammed treasure box it was when Harold Nicolson (the writer, husband of Vita Sackville-West of Sissinghurst fame, and nephew of the 1st Marquess of Dufferin and Ava) described it nearly a century ago. He wrote of the Clandeboye hall in *Helen's Tower* (1937), his tribute to his uncle:

"The steps which led down to the front door were flanked by a double row of curling stones from Scotland and from Canada [where Dufferin had been Governor General]...

"To the left of these unwieldy playthings stood an enormous block of Egyptian granite carved with the semblance of the cow-headed Hathor and bearing the ibis cartouche of Thutmosis I. Balanced upon this pink monolith was the stuffed and startled head of a rhinoceros.

"In the plaster of the left wall were embedded a series of Greek inscriptions picked out in red paint...

"Beyond these inscriptions, a Russian bear reared enormous paws. On the right hand of the entrance, a mummy case, two cannon, a Burmese bell slung between carved figures and a second bear of smaller dimensions were artistically grouped.

"The wall behind them had been covered with wire netting on which were affixed dirks, daggers, cutlasses, pistols, lances, curling brooms and a collection of those neat little fly-whisks with which the acolytes dust the high altar of St Peter's at Rome."

Lindy preserved all this while creating a future. She restored the woodland in line with the plans of the 1st Marquess's landscape gardener, James Frazer. She renovated and redecorated the 12 main bedrooms at Clandeboye. But she also created a new one.

With her friends Julian and Bojana Reilly, she built the Cairo Room on the site of the old Museum Room in 2002. And she was determined to make it a spectacular.

The tent was made by Tariq al Fattouh, a Cairo tent-maker from the Khayyamiyya, the Tent-makers' Bazaar – the last remaining covered bazaar in Islamic Cairo (the others have all succumbed to fire or general decay over the years). It was, Julian Reilly reports, "the finest tent he had ever made".

Julian adds, "The income from the tent – the biggest project Tariq had ever undertaken, and which he had done during the hot and therefore quiet summer months, when the absence of tourists means only a trickle of income to most – had in fact enabled him finally to get married!"

And what a splendid, ginormous tent it is – 24 yards of red and white roofed tent wall, decorated with Pharaonic and Islamic designs.

One of the many remarkable things about Lindy was that she would do utterly remarkable things – like taking Cairo to Northern Ireland – and it didn't seem unusual at the time. You were so used to her constant ideas. Now that she's dead, you have the immediate benefit of hind-sight – and realise how exceptional it all was.

She brought a painterly eye to Clandeboye's renovations and innovations. That eye remembered Lindy's first view of Clandeboye when she went in 1962, two years before her marriage to Sheridan. On her first morning there, she woke "to see a magnificent, inter-locking landscape of greens that led down to a lake. It was particularly beautiful: there were low, horizontal bands of Irish mist, allowing only certain parts of the landscape to be sharply defined; those mists that hung over the lake have a Japanese watercolour quality."

In 2019, not long before she died, she installed the abstract stained-glass windows – the Sheridan Windows – she'd designed for the Clandeboye Chapel. It was all thanks to an idea from the writer Rupert Sheldrake, with direction from the art expert Thierry Morel about the simplicity of the colours.

She wrote in her diary in 2019, "The windows have fitted in most endearingly and I'm so thankful that I've done them – they were like a kaleidoscope… They make the chapel much more holy."

Her windows figured prominently on the desperately sad day of her funeral just over a year later. As her friend Professor Jane Ohlmeyer of Trinity College Dublin said, "The funeral service was very moving (even for those of us joining remotely), especially towards the end, as the sunlight streamed in through Lindy's exquisite, blue stained-glass windows."

In her diary, Lindy did ponder writing a book called *The Morphing of a Great Estate*. But Lindy was never smug about her improvements to Clandeboye or her possessions.

Once, leafing through the books in the Clandeboye library, I came across a book on Troy by Heinrich Schliemann, the German archaeologist who'd discovered the site of Troy in the 19th century. To my astonishment, there was a letter stuffed inside the book from Schliemann to the 1st Marquess, written in ancient Greek.

I rushed to Lindy, full of smug pride at finding the letter and my ability to read the Greek. She was interested from a historical point of view – but she never showed any of that distasteful pride herself in her considerable possessions and achievements.

That's why I felt this book should be put together in Lindy's honour. In part, it was to remember her painting, her mercurial nature, and her gifts for sweet kindness and uniquely funny conversation.

But this book is also to remember the way she reacted to the deep tragedy of Sheridan's early death – and what she did at Clandeboye.

She was always completely open about Sheridan's death: that he'd had AIDS; that he'd had gay affairs. She talked often about his bravery: how he'd never complained for a second as he lay dying; how he'd said to her that, after he was gone, "You can sell Clandeboye but I'd much rather if you didn't."

After a period of intense grief after Sheridan died, Lindy took up painting again with renewed verve and originality. It's like the Old Testament story of the honey in the beehive that grew inside the dead lion – captured on the tin of Tate & Lyle golden syrup: "Out of the strong came forth sweetness."

You might say something similar about that tricky childhood: out of the unkindness came kindness.

As she wrote in her diary, "I can remember Mummy in 1959 in Granny's bedroom, saying I was useless and should do something – it was her who kept pushing me – thank you, Mum. I wish I could have been closer to you."

The cruelty of her mother was replaced by Sheridan's kindness, as she recorded in her diary:

"Sheridan has allowed me to be exactly what I wanted to be. He knew that I had in me the desire to be like I am at this moment. If he had lived, I could not have been like this.

"Did he die because of me? That is a huge, vast question. If he was alive now, what would he say? 'Dear,

I love you. That is all you need to know.' Then he would go back to reading a bridge puzzle. It was a wonderful mind – and he really loved me – he could see me now – perhaps he can – if so, I would evaporate into his arms – not for sex or power but just to be like him. He was not vain like me. I'm always checking what I look like or thinking about how I appear. He never did. He was himself. I never achieved this. Ho, ho, I'm not dead. So I still can – and I will."

How she threw herself into Clandeboye, turning it into a hive of activity: less social, though she did host endless gatherings, than charitable and commercial.

She revived Clandeboye's fortunes. Every year – every month, it seemed – there was a new scheme: the anaerobic digester, the spectacular success of Clandeboye Yoghurt; the forest school; the Conservation Volunteers; ventures with Kew Gardens; the sprouting of new gardens and ripping out of old features (as her head gardener Fergus Thompson writes in this book); filming on the estate. She was always devising new ingenious ways to make the whole place useful.

In her diary in 2018, she wrote, "I always wanted to be born a man because I hated having to play the part of a female – now I have this all by accident. I love it."

***

Her furious activity extended beyond Clandeboye. In 2019, she had the idea of bringing sheep back to Hampstead Heath, inspired by paintings by Constable showing cattle grazing on the Heath in the 1820s and

30s. Two Oxford Downs and three Norfolk Horns – rare breeds – were duly brought on the Heath by the City of London Corporation, which owns it.

She felt that serious things could be achieved, even if – or especially if – you were enjoying yourself. She wrote in her diary:

"If there is laughter and joy, however serious the business at hand, you create more than if it is too heavy-handed and serious. Fun is serious – it's the best thing to have fun and to play makes one creative and one makes things that one had no idea were possible."

Her business ideas were many and varied. Some didn't prosper but, more often than not, they were resounding successes. She particularly liked the deal where she managed to get BT to restore Helen's Tower in return for installing a telephone mast there.

Her nephew Sheridan Guinness recalls, "The deal shows her backbone and principle – and that big companies can be good and do good, given a little direction."

She was intensely interested in politics, particularly Northern Irish politics. But she played a blinder in never cleaving to one side or the other. In 2000, she had political councillors of all shades over to tea at Clandeboye to hand over a wood to the country. Still she rose above any local politics. She didn't ban political chats – far from it – but you wouldn't have known which way she leaned.

I think she was reacting to the frivolity of that unhappy youth; flung from yacht to yacht; from the smart set in London to golf lessons with Ben Hogan in Palm Beach (she retained an elegant, slow golf swing into her late

70s); surrounded by the beautiful and the damned – and the extremely idle.

"Her mother was more interested in poodles," says Viscount Gage, a friend of Lindy's since 1954. "Lindy could have been a poor little rich girl, shuffled across the Atlantic with lawyers, with two angry parents."

Instead, she recoiled against that cold, unhappy time and developed an unusual capacity for warm empathy.

Nicky Gage adds, "Lindy had so many sides to her character, including the rarest of all qualities: being able to put herself in someone else's place."

It also meant she was extremely shrewd at working out your character. In her diary, she correctly said of my tennis (not too bad in the knock-up; terrible in a real game): "Harry is too neurotic to be a good tennis-player."

She had a sixth sense for working out what you were thinking. She once ticked me off for being polite in a chilly way to a pompous but well-meaning soul, also staying at Clandeboye.

"You think you're more intelligent than him, don't you?" she said.

"I didn't realise it was so obvious," I said, chastened.

I still don't think it was obvious – except to figures like Lindy with extra-sensory perception for what people were really like, equipped with those X-ray specs to see through the fronts we all put up.

Her great friend Christopher Balfour, the former Chairman of Christie's, said of her powers of perception, "Lindy really understood her contemporaries – Francis Bacon and Lucian Freud wouldn't have seen her if she didn't see them eye to eye."

The architectural historian Robert O'Byrne remembers that she could be an "imperious hostess" because she knew how people tended to behave and the best way to corral them. He recalls "being ordered to remain in the library while she showed visitors around the house – 'Otherwise, darling, you'll only correct me when I say something wrong.' The confinement was eased by well-stocked bookshelves and an equally well-stocked drinks table."

That capacity for hyper-perception was that much more remarkable given the deafness that intensified in middle age. She got very good at lip-reading and interpreting what people were saying by their body language.

"I can tell the exact moment a man telling an anecdote expects you to laugh at the punchline," she said. She was also very skilled at never saying "What?", knowing that it only broke the anecdotalist's flow and annoyed them.

Deafness was a particular cruelty in someone so curious. Robert O'Byrne remembers her "insatiable curiosity about everyone else (chronically deaf, she habitually quizzed friends about their private lives in a very loud voice)".

She fully embraced the possibility of a cochlear implant and calmly accepted the possibility of it going very badly wrong. When it went right, and her hearing improved dramatically, she proclaimed happily to the world about the electronic device implanted inside her head, "I've become a cyborg!"

She delighted on saying when she turned on the implant, "I've put my ears in."

The Marquess of Cholmondeley says, "I remember

vividly Lindy's exhilaration following her ear implant operation – it really was like a blind person being given back their sight. Suddenly she could enjoy music again and have a conversation without having to lip-read. One realised what a nightmare her deafness had been."

***

Lindy also reacted against the lazy, lotus-eating lives she had witnessed growing up.

Her London housekeeper, Ana Gama, once answered the door early in the morning to find an important business visitor. She rushed upstairs to find Lindy sound asleep, having forgotten the appointment.

Rather than going downstairs and admit to over-sleeping, Lindy got dressed, lightning-quick, dashed downstairs, slipped out of the front door, unnoticed, with her unwitting visitor waiting in the sitting room. She then turned around on the doorstep, came rushing back in, slammed the door and ran to her visitor, with profuse apologies – she'd had another meeting that had overrun, she said.

Her allergy to self-indulgence guided her towards charity. When she sold a Lucian Freud picture (Freud had been married to Sheridan's sister, the writer Caroline Blackwood), she used the proceeds to endow her charitable foundation to help the forest school in the Clandeboye woods:

"[I went to the] Lucian Freud show – My little picture is there. It held its own – it was generating all those children in the woods: I find this thrilling. I could have bought a house in Portugal and could be there now but I would not be happy and fulfilled as I feel this morning." – Diary entry, 2019.

That same year, Lindy wrote in her diary, "How wonderful if Clandeboye can continue as a great beacon of success – not a palace for the rich but a blissful health area of forests and land loved by the local communities and making a financial contribution both to itself and society at large with creative public access but no commercialisation nor mass tourism.

"Clandeboye hopefully will have corners where I am in spirit. I have no desire for memorials."

***

Lindy could dip back into that gilded world perfectly happily and talk to anyone in it with ease, deafness notwithstanding. "I can be smart!" she'd declare after she'd raced upstairs to get changed into a chic jacket, doing it all in five minutes.

But, perhaps as a reaction to the clothes-obsessed Swans of Fifth Avenue, among whom she'd grown up, she was much happier in long shorts, trainers, T-shirt, bodywarmer and tennis visor.

"For painting, I stick on such an unbelievably awful combination of clothes that I'd be ashamed to be seen in them by anybody," she told the *Sunday Times* in 2009. "It usually involves shorts and a pair of big socks."

She had a completely straightforward, pragmatic approach to clothes. One morning, she came to her housekeeper, Ana Gama, bearing a pair of very smart trousers in her hands.

"Today, we're going to make shorts," Lindy said, handing over the trousers.

"Under the knee?" said Ana.

"Just on the knee," Lindy said, leaving Ana to chop up the grand trousers.

As Ana recounts in this book, Lindy was delighted one day when, shopping with her near Holland Villas Road, a passing man offered her £20, thinking she was a tramp.

Her friend Sophie Hicks says, "Lindy loved to behave like a ragamuffin. I loved that she was rough at the edges and at the same time lived in a gilded world."

Lindy was really happiest in those clothes, for painting and for running round Clandeboye and London. What she really yearned for was to paint and to make Clandeboye useful.

***

For all the jokes, Lindy could be very serious in conversation. Her seriousness was rooted in deep reading. Every night, after dinner, she would read the *Financial Times* and the *Telegraph*, and books of a high philosophical and spiritual quality. At the time of her death, she was reading a biography of the artist Roger Fry by Virginia Woolf.

Her diaries are well-written, full of direct, original thought and funny. And she paid wise heed to the advice given her by her friend, writer Robert Kee, in 1974: "A diary must be full of gossip – that is what in time evokes the period."

For all her wit, she led a high-minded life. She very rarely watched television. "Will you come round one evening," she said one day in London, "and teach me how to watch television?"

That was one of her completely self-aware, mock-Marie Antoinette lines.

As well as painting obsessively, she read about painters and painting in depth, as she recorded in her diary:

"Delacroix said you should be able to paint a picture of a man falling from a 4th storey before he lands! I think there is something in speed."

Her reading was much higher-brow than anything I or most people read. She felt a burning desire to learn – she minded not being educated at university or a good school.

Her friend Anne Lambton says that, as a result, she was "an eternal student". In 1964, shortly before she married at twenty-three, Lindy wrote in her diary, "How can one become educated at this late stage? My idea is to try and find a teacher who could give private lessons."

But, as the 1st Marquess's biographer, Andrew Gailey, says, that lack of formal education "produced a freedom and a wit and a hunger for all roads of thought".

She once told Gailey, "I'm not prepared for a modern world. I've been trained for a world that was lost."

It was certainly true that staying at Clandeboye was like breathing the enchantments of a vanished age: a great, comfortable country house, stuffed with intriguing people, tucked inside its own estate, set apart from the world, where you were waited on, hand and foot.

In a farewell to Lindy after her death, her cousin Sabrina Stoppard (née Guinness) recalls her first stay at Clandeboye: "I remember first meeting you and Sheridan when we were children and I just think of the whirlwind you brought with you. And the giggles and the excitement of our first visit to Clandeboye: the old records, the dancing, the frolicking, the tennis, Helen's Tower."

In a 1973 diary entry, Lindy described the breathless life of a Clandeboye weekend: "Tennis, shooting, chairs, conversation, paper games and extraordinary corridor creeping were among the non-stop activities." (I'm not sure what "chairs" means.)

Clandeboye had certainly changed since the days of *Great Granny Webster* (1977), the fictional portrayal of the house by Caroline Blackwood, Sheridan's sister. At Dunmartin Hall, as Clandeboye was called in the book, "the food at meals was always stone cold because it had to be carried by the butler from a dungeon kitchen... There was very rarely hot water and it was considered a luxury if anyone managed to get a peat-brown trickle of a bath."

The holes in the roof "could only be kept at bay by pieces of dangling string which helped direct the massive flow of uncountable leaks to the various pots and pans and jam jars in which it suited my family that they should land".

Caroline's sister, Lady Perdita Blackwood, says her sister was using poetic licence – Clandeboye was in rather good nick in the war, she remembers.

Clandeboye under Sheridan and Lindy may have

belonged to an earlier age of entertaining. But it never felt fogeyish or consciously old-fashioned; quite the opposite, with Lindy and Sheridan's eye and hunger for the new.

At Clandeboye, Lindy was daring in mixing the generations and people from different worlds. Francis Russell, the Christie's Old Masters specialist, says, "She told me that I was a pollinator. I asked what she meant and she said I was good at mixing and introducing people. If anyone mastered that art, it was her, as weekends at Clandeboye and parties in London proved."

It must be said that the pollinating didn't always come off. One weekend in the mid-1970s, Lindy invited the great American poet Robert Lowell, married to her sister-in-law, Caroline Blackwood. Also staying were several hearty types, there for the Clandeboye shoot.

In her customary, enthusiastic way, Lindy arranged for Lowell to give a poetry reading on Saturday evening in the library. The hearties availed themselves of the drinks tray and took their places beside Lindy as the great man of American letters began his recital.

"And, one by one, these brutes in their shooting socks tiptoed out of the room to go and have a drink," said Lindy. "By the time he finished, only Caroline and I were left in the room."

Lindy was both modern and other-worldly. The Tennyson poem commissioned by the 1st Marquess for Helen's Tower has a terrific line: "Love is in and out of time." Lindy was in and out of her time.

What she did at Clandeboye was astonishing. She did it for the people of Northern Ireland. She wrote in her diary in 2019, "Living in Ulster is like being in a vast family – adorable."

She did it, too, for adored Sheridan. She has left behind a monument to Northern Ireland and to Sheridan. Her energy, style and selfless devotion were enormous.

I utterly adored her. Her death has left me bereft.

Her death leaves a huge hole, too, in County Down. Just off the road between Belfast and Bangor, my dear godmother did irreplaceable things for me – and all around her, for miles in every direction.

LINDY'S LEGACY

Thomas Pakenham

*Thomas Pakenham is a leading historian and tree expert.
Among his books are* Meetings with Remarkable Trees,
The Boer War *and* The Scramble for Africa. *He lives
at Tullynally Castle in County Westmeath, Ireland.*
*A great friend of Lindy's, he gave the address at her
2021 memorial service in St Margaret's, Westminster.*

I shall never forget my first meeting with Lindy. It
was in the winter of 1964, soon after her marriage to
Sheridan. My wife Valerie and I had been invited to a
glamorous weekend for newlyweds at Russborough, the
Beits' Palladian retreat in County Wicklow.

Alfred Beit, our host, was most welcoming. But he
made it clear which of the couples were the stars. "Lindy
and Sheridan will join the guns," said our written
instructions. "Valerie and Thomas will walk the dogs."

Lindy and Sheridan were certainly a dazzling couple
and already celebrities in London. But I wonder if
Lindy knew then that, as well as marrying a rich and
handsome peer, she was marrying a garden.

In fact, Lindy was to be the last in the line of five
energetic chatelaines who created and changed and
transformed not only the garden but the whole landscape at Clandeboye.

Their names read like a drum-roll: Dorcas, Helen, Brenda, Maureen, Lindy. Today the first four are hardly more than names attached to parts of the estate: Dorcas's garden by the chapel, Helen's Tower in the demesne, Brenda's woodland garden, Maureen's garden with the Moon Gate. But Lindy's masterful presence still dominates the whole world of Clandeboye.

Early in spring 2021 – shortly after Lindy's death – protected by my two Pfizer jabs, I went up to Clandeboye to talk and exchange memories with her veteran head gardener, Fergus Thompson.

They were a perfect match, Lindy and Fergus. They worked together for 23 years: Lindy, hyperactive, a sun-loving plant and a brilliant painter-gardener, always intent on opening up and clarifying the landscape: Fergus, introspective, a master-plantsman, and the spirit of the woods, handsome, bearded, mysterious.

But, on that spring day, Fergus and I both felt overwhelmed by Lindy's death. Indeed it was hard to believe she was not somewhere ahead of us in the garden, trowel in one hand, paintbrush in the other.

Soon we came to Brenda's Garden, now much more elegant than I remembered it, with five waterfalls sculpted out of the heavy clay, and a triple-headed Cappadocian maple.

"There's the champion Embothrium," I said, delighted that this scarlet giant from Chile had survived the most recent storm, the vicious storm-girl Ophelia, "and there's the famous handkerchief tree. Do you know the story of that tree?"

I explained that I was staying at Clandeboye in the late 1990s, when Lindy invited a party of international dendrologists to visit the garden. They were no doubt a serious-minded lot – somewhat stuffy, I imagined. So I had slipped out before breakfast to enrich the young handkerchief tree with the contents of a packet of Kleenex.

"Look," I cried, running ahead of the party, "the handkerchief tree has begun to flower."

Lindy was completely fooled. Her eyes shone with excitement. Then the penny dropped. She flew at me, knocked me to the ground, and we rolled over and over down the bank. The dendrologists couldn't believe their eyes. Behaving like a teenager – and she a *marchioness*! Fergus gave a wry smile.

We next visited the pinetum created by the 1st Marquess, and his devoted wife Harriot. I knew the place well – or thought I did. It was a strange idea, this Victorian fashion for concentrating all the conifers in one place, with no deciduous trees, like oaks and maples, to provide contrast. Not an idea that I think was often successful. And the Clandeboye version had proved an ill-omened example.

The 1st Marquess was exceptionally rich in talent. As a diplomat and proconsul, he had brought peace to numerous troubled lands. He had served as ambassador in half the capitals of Europe, and was acknowledged by Queen Victoria as one of the pillars of her empire.

But how to control his own expenditure was apparently beyond him. Soon he began to mortgage his estates in order to pay for his reckless spending on garden and

"Mummy spotted it. I'm like a pony that hasn't been broken in – still as wild as I was as a child." Lindy Guinness, aged 3, 1944, by Hugh Joseph Riddle.

Below: "Sheridan and Clandeboye are my legacy – not what I have done but what I've made possible for others to do." Clandeboye, originally called Ballyleidy, was settled by the Dufferins' ancestors, the Blackwoods, in the early 17th century. The house, built in 1804 by Robert Woodgate, was remodelled later in the 19th century by the 1st Marquess, who named it Clandeboye.

Photograph by Christopher Sykes, 1999.

Newly married: Sheridan and Lindy Dufferin by David Hockney, Holland Villas Road, 1964.

Lindy Dufferin as the Old Lady, in a headscarf. Elisabeth Luard, *far right*, as the Boy, in Edward Elgar's *Wand of Youth*, Lawnside School, 1956.

Girl in Pearls: Lindy, 18, in *Country Life*, 1959.

Portrait of the Artist as a Young Woman: Lindy Guinness, 19, 1960.

Bloomsbury life: Lindy's sketch of her bedroom at Charleston, East Sussex, while staying with mentor Duncan Grant, 1962.

Wedding of the Year: Sheridan Dufferin and Lindy Guinness, Westminster Abbey, 1964.

Lindy by Duncan Grant, 1962.

On honeymoon in America: Lindy and
Sheridan Dufferin on a plane, 1964.

… and David Hockney came, too.

Lindy skating in the American
Midwest, 1964.

Hockney beheaded: John
Kasmin, Hockney, Lindy
and Sheridan on a
Hollywood film set, 1964.

Artist's
Model
Number
One: Lindy
by David
Hockney,
1966.

Artist's Model
Number Two:
Lindy by John
Craxton, 1966.

Ossie Clark wearing a Fair Isle sweater, by David Hockney, 1970.

Celia Birtwell by David Hockney, 1977. The fashion designers Ossie Clark (1942–96) and Celia Birtwell (b.1941) were central figures in the Swinging Sixties, painted by Hockney in *Mr and Mrs Clark and Percy* (1971). They were friends of Sheridan and Lindy, who bought these two pictures.

Lindy by George Deene, 1967.

Opposite L: "For Sheridan & Lindy – a thank you note, love from David H Dec 1969 proof 1/1".

Opposite R: The real thing: the armchair in the Clandeboye library.

Friends reunited: David Hockney paints Lindy…
And the finished product: Lindy by Hockney, 2002.

A Royal Visit: Prince Charles comes to Clandeboye, 1999. Left to right: Roger Garvan, Robin Manley, Billy McKee, Fergus Thompson, Barry Garvan, John Robertson, John Craig, Lola Armstrong, Robert John Cousins, Len McLean, Dick Blakiston-Houston, John Witchell, Elaine Graham, Mark Logan, Jackie Shields, Olive McLean, Ruth Roulston, Alex Mantell, Nick Lindsay.

Lindy and the Namibian, 2007, by Thomas Pakenham. Thomas says, "She had just drawn his portrait under the shade of a colossal baobab – possibly the largest in southern Africa."

tower and lake. No doubt Harriot did her best to control things. But his end was tragic enough. (Appropriately, his second son, Basil Blackwood, was the illustrator for Belloc's *Cautionary Tales*.)

Desperate for money, the 1ˢᵗ Marquess took the chairmanship of what proved to be a crooked mining company. Its chief executive, Whitaker Wright, was prosecuted for swindling his shareholders. Wright committed suicide in style: he took arsenic in the dock. The 1ˢᵗ Marquess lost still more money (he, too, was a shareholder) and died a broken man.

So the Clandeboye Pinetum, as I remembered, was only too graphic a symbol of the humiliation of its creator. Californian giants – noble firs and redwoods – were clogged with ivy. Where was the champion willow podocarpus? It had vanished into the nettles. Many of the great trees had been decapitated decades earlier, but no one had bothered to move the corpses.

Then Lindy arrived. At first, I think, even Lindy paled at the thought of dealing with all this wreckage. But deal she did. By the end of the '90s, she had arranged with Fergus that the pinetum should be fully restored. It has been a long and fraught process.

Fergus admitted that he wasn't in "complete agreement with Lady Dufferin" about the need to remove all the corpses. Of course it's now commonplace to see dead trees left behind to feed the living beetles. But tidiness was a red line for Lindy. Lorry-loads of corpses were removed, and a tidy new path system begun.

You can now cross the stream without a risk to your life. And many new conifers have been planted: rarities like the Huon Pine from Tasmania, Southern Beech and Totaras from New Zealand, and the cypress-like Fitzroya, named after the Antarctic explorer, Captain Fitzroy, who first introduced Darwin to the secrets of evolution.

As Fergus and I wandered back across the demesne, we exchanged memories of how Lindy's gift for mischief would sometimes prove embarrassing.

Now Lindy had recently restored Helen's Tower, the slim Gothic eye-catcher created by the 1st Marquess for his mother. It was – and is – an elegant rival to the bigger and cruder Scrabo Tower, built by the Blackwoods' political rivals, the Stewart family. This faces Newtownards, a few miles south of Clandeboye.

Once restored, Helen's Tower was one of Lindy's favourite lunch spots. It meant carrying the lunch four stories up a winding staircase. But the butler, Robert John, took this in his stride.

I remember once having lunch there accompanied by a theatrical thunderstorm. How Lindy's own eyes flashed in unison with the lightning! "And what a privilege it is for me," she told us four men, "to be here with the two most interesting men in Europe."

Each of us four men then looked round, nursing the same unspoken question. Who was the *other* most interesting man in Europe?

On another occasion, when I lunched there with Lindy, the four guests included the distinguished director of Kew Gardens, Sir Peter Crane, and two young friends of mine, a South African journalist and an exceedingly pretty young girl, called Catherine. It was unusually hot as we trekked back to the house.

"What about a skinny dip?" said Lindy, when we came to a large pond surrounded by sycamores and oaks.

"*Must* we really?" asked Sir Peter.

"I am afraid we must, sir," said the journalist.

The men gingerly removed their clothes at one end of the pond, the ladies demurely at the other – and both parties converged at the middle. The water was up to our chests, which was a relief.

"You're cheating, Peter," I said, somewhat cheekily, "you're wearing your spectacles."

"And *I've* got my hearing-aids on," said Lindy.

I was first back to the shore, and (I blush to admit it) took some long shots with my zoom lens. That evening, as I was changing for dinner, there was a knock on the door.

It was Robert John, the butler. "Skinny dip, skinny dip," he muttered in his rich Ulster brogue. "Can I see the photos of the skinny dip?" Somehow the word had already got round.

But there was another side to Lindy when it came to gardening. Fergus explained to me how seriously they would debate the future of some important tree or other plant (Fergus writes in detail about these debates in his chapter in this book):

"She had the attitude that if the plant wasn't doing very well, even if it was a very special plant, it could just be removed... She'd say, 'We'll *McIlhenny* this one.' It was one of her favourite expressions."

Henry McIlhenny was the American millionaire who'd created the famous garden at Glenveagh and was known for his ruthless treatment of plants.

I questioned Fergus closely on this point. Was Lindy really so ruthless? And how good was her judgement?

Fergus told me that she was often right. One plant, a fine Zelkova, was digging in to a beautiful Metasequoia. So the Zelkova had to go. At other times, he would disagree with her: "She took out plants that she found offensive because of the colour of their flowers – because they clashed, for instance."

She also removed many trees in order to open up the landscape. Fergus showed me a great rarity, a Thujopsis dolabrata, which Lindy had planned to cut down because it blocked a view of the chapel. "She put it on death row, while we argued about its future."

This was a few months before her own death in October. A scheme of Lindy's which was hotly debated was the removal of a castellated beech hedge planted by her mother-in-law, Maureen the Dowager Marchioness, in the 1950s.

Maureen had put it there to protect her sparkling new mixed border of lilies and primulas. Lindy first insisted that the castellated hedge should be lowered in order to open up the view of the pleasure grounds from the Chapel Walk. It would also put an end to the ground elder. Fergus was dubious. The hedge was lowered, but the ground elder grew better than ever. "Then Lady Dufferin decided, 'No, we are not going to tolerate this hedge, we want it out, we want to get rid of the ground elder.' So the whole damn lot was dug out."

I suspect Lindy was not sorry to see the humiliating end of Maureen's hedge. Lindy was only human, and

Maureen proved a difficult mother-in-law, to put it mildly. At one time (according to the story told me by her elder daughter, Caroline), Maureen lost her wits and insisted her staff addressed her as Her Royal Highness. She was convinced she was the Queen Mother.

She soon recovered, but Lindy found Maureen's visits to Clandeboye hard to stomach. Of course, Lindy was well aware that it was Maureen who had saved Clandeboye from disaster, buying it back twice from the banks to which it was mortgaged, using her own Guinness money.

But Maureen found mischief of any kind irresistible. I remember Lindy showing me two stone slabs which Maureen had erected on a small island on the edge of the lake. The first was a memorial for the life of John Maude, Maureen's third husband. (She herself had reverted to the title acquired from her first husband, the 4th Marquess, Sheridan's father, killed in action in Burma in 1945.)

The second slab was a eulogy to herself, then very much alive. "What happened to those slabs?" I asked Lindy when I next visited the island on the edge of the lake. There was no sign of either. "Oh, those slabs. I threw them in the lake."

Sometimes the two marchionesses would overlap amicably at a weekend at Clandeboye. And then on Monday warfare would resume. In the late '80s, there was a protracted court case in London, involving millions of pounds buried in Guinness family trusts, and Lindy and Maureen were on opposite sides. Rather to my surprise, it was Maureen who won.

Meanwhile Fergus had taken me to see other radical changes in the garden and demesne created by Lindy – changes of which he entirely approved. The first was a new wild garden, beyond Brenda's Garden, dedicated to the memory of Sheridan. It's a romantic retreat, a glade carved out of an old quarry and filled with rare plants from China and the Himalayas (some of which, I'm proud to say, I gave her myself).

The second radical alteration was right at the front gate. It was there that Maureen had planted a new avenue of scarlet-flowered horse chestnuts. They had grown well, too well in Lindy's view, a dreary tunnel among the billowing oaks and beech. Lindy gave them the McIlhenny treatment. They were replaced with a new avenue of young oaks, now 30 feet high. Lindy dealt equally briskly with Maureen's attention-seeking cherries dotting the lawns and masking the kitchen wing.

And Lindy's masterstroke, I think, was the small sub-tropical planting immediately opposite the front door: a painterly composition of spiky New Zealand flax and towering Cordylines, topped up with splashes of pink rhododendrons. And, best of all, two magnificent evergreen magnolias crowning the front door.

"Great work," I said to Fergus. Then I remembered how two of my own prize magnolias were stolen from my garden at Tullynally in County Westmeath 12 years before, and who were the thieves in this infamous business.

It happened one evening in late November. I was down in our walled garden, potting plants, when I saw a shadowy figure slip in through the gate. To my astonishment, he took out a spade and began to dig up one of my most precious small evergreens, a Magnolia delavayi that I had reared from seed I had collected in Yunnan.

"What on earth are you doing?" I cried.

"Orders from Lady Dufferin," said the shadowy figure in a strong Ulster brogue. And I recognised Fergus. "She said you had promised her two of your best magnolias."

"Stop," I cried. "I certainly didn't give that promise."

The shadowy figure continued to dig.

"Stop, stop," I said. But soon both magnolias were dug up and then loaded into the van.

Of course I should have guessed what would happen. It was men like Fergus who defied King James at the siege of Derry. It was men like Fergus who gave King Billy his kingdom. What hope had I of saving my prize magnolias?

But this story has a happy ending. Fergus had taken two of my four remaining magnolias. In the privileged climate of Clandeboye (it's a couple of miles from the sea), the two stolen trees grew to perfection. Even the worst winters couldn't destroy them. The two left at Tullynally were not so fortunate. They were both killed by the great frosts of 2010.

I told Fergus that he – and Lindy – were both now forgiven. But I am still waiting for cuttings from my long-lost prize magnolias.

Lindy shooting in the 1960s.

Lawnside School – NOT the
Best Days of Our Lives

Elisabeth Luard

Elisabeth Luard is a food-writer and Cookery Correspondent for the Oldie *magazine. She is the author of* My Life as a Wife: Love, Liquor and What to Do About the Other Women.

I last caught up with Lindy Guinness – artist, yoghurt entrepreneur and the Marchioness of Dufferin and Ava – when she hosted the *Oldie* Magazine Summer Party in 2019.

It was in tandem with the opening of her latest exhibition of Irish landscapes (mostly with cows, "the ladies", generous providers of raw material for her highly successful yoghurt business).

I was at school with Lindy at Lawnside – boarding, girls-only – in the bleak Malvern Hills. Both of us were a bit foreign in fifties Britain, even though Lawnside served as a last ditch for those who'd blotted their copybooks at other schools. We'd both travelled abroad and might even have been able to speak a language other than our own.

We were taught English (Shakespeare, Jane Austen), Latin (Virgil; no Catullus – far too sexy), the history of empire and mathematics up to a point where we might be able to tackle the household accounts. No science – perish the thought. Throughout my school-days, I never admitted to fluency in Spanish and French – the result of a diplomatic stepfather – or to spending holidays abroad. It was probably worse for Lindy, as one or other of her parents was always in the tabloids, and word got around.

The main school excitement – a scandal that even made the London papers – in the four years we were incarcerated was an unexplained decision that we were not permitted to fraternise with other years or take walks on the Malvern Hills in pairs. Three was company; two was not. Word went round that the edict had something to do with the English mistress, Miss Dillon Weston (later cited as an inspirational teacher by novelist Angela Huth) and the sudden departure of a sixth-former known to have attended Miss DW's coffee evenings in the attic.

Miss DW wore a hairy tweed suit and socks with brogues. Only Miss DW's special pupils were invited to the attic. Lindy was. I was not.

On the other hand, Lindy and I were both special favourites of Lady Aske, the art mistress, a war widow obliged to teach for a living (as she would explain to us sadly) – a gentle soul who encouraged both her star pupils, Lindy and me, to work on very expensive water-colour paper she bought for us herself. I found this a terrible responsibility – maybe Lindy did, too. Maybe neither of us ever lost that feeling of "What if I make a mess?" that accompanies every new sheet of paper pinned to the board.

Certainly, when we walked round her exhibition

together at the summer party, Lindy seemed as anxious and uncertain of her talent as when we were schoolgirls all those years ago.

She loved acting, as did I. We were on stage together for a performance of Edward Elgar's *The Wand of Youth*, a combination of speaking and dancing that suited some of us better than others. Lindy played the Old Lady, an important speaking part, while I starred as the Boy with the Wand of Youth.

Neither of our mothers showed up for the event, though we both featured in *Tatler*. Parental approval was never granted, even when earned. Lindy's mother, it seemed to me even at the time, was as careless of her daughter's happiness as was mine.

In later years, our paths crossed infrequently, but we were always glad to see each other at events such as an anniversary gathering of debutantes who came out in the same year ('59, since you ask). Neither of us were successful in the main purpose of our year as a deb – attracting a proposal of marriage from a suitable young man of whom our families approved. Preferably an English duke in need of a dowry to repair the roof.

Thereafter, our lives took very different paths. I had married satirist-about-Soho Nicholas Luard, engaged in subversive anti-Establishment activities, including the proprietorship of *Private Eye* at the time when the paper was sued for libel by Randolph Churchill.

The following year, 1964, Lindy glided down the aisle in Westminster Abbey with Sheridan Dufferin, possessor of a title, estate and fortune, already a well-known art-connoisseur who'd just started a London gallery with his friend and fellow party-animal John Kasmin. As an eccentric and generous hostess, she divided a glamorous life between her husband's ancestral home in Northern Ireland and a splendid mansion in Holland Park.

Our husbands met just once, as I remember, at a dinner party in Chester Square thrown by glamorous political hostess Pamela Egremont – and hated each other at first sight. Exchanges became so heated (no, I can't remember what it was all about) that Nicholas, rather grandly, invited Lindy to take her husband home.

We grew up together. Our mothers were girlhood friends, which meant I often spent weekends when my diplomatic family was elsewhere at Lindy's mother's second husband's country estate in Rutland. Lindy's mother, as mine, was a spoilt beauty – born Lady Isabel Manners, she was a daughter of the Duke of Rutland, brought up at Belvoir Castle – and our mothers met during the pre-war London season.

Lindy's father, playboy financier Loel Guinness, based in Florida, was the subject of many a late-night, tearful discussion when Lindy felt she'd failed to live up to the intelligence of her brothers or the beauty of her step-mother, Gloria.

Matching tears came from my own realisation that my mother, equally rich and spoilt and able to choose who and what she wanted, had lost interest in the two children of a wartime marriage she'd rather forget.

On one of these weekend respites from school, Lindy's stepfather, Bobby Throckmorton, chased me round the box-hedges (I was just 14) in an attempt at seduction. I never complained or told a grown-up, but Lindy and

I discussed the event enthusiastically and thought it rather funny.

O tempora, o mores.

Rest in peace, old friend. I'll miss you at the next (and possibly last) gathering of the debutante class of '59.

A Bigger Splash at Holland Villas Road

David Hockney

David Hockney is one of the world's greatest living artists. He studied at the Royal College of Art (1959–62), where his work was spotted by Sheridan Dufferin and John Kasmin (known as Kasmin), who both ran the Kasmin Gallery on Bond Street. He was a friend of Lindy's for nearly sixty years.

Kasmin started buying pieces of mine when I was in my second year at the Royal College of Art.

So, by my last year, I was quite a rich student – I could buy cigarettes in packets of 20, not 10. Sheridan was Kasmin's partner and I had my first exhibition there in December 1963. Lindy was 79 when she died – a bit younger than me. She complained about my smoking but, anyway, I'm 85…

I have known Lindy since 1962. She was always a painter. She had a proper artist's studio with a north light, I remember. It was in Kensington somewhere.

When she married Sheridan, they bought a grand house in Holland Villas Road, where she had a studio on the top floor – again with a north light. The reason artists had north-windowed studios is that then the shadows don't change. They had forgotten this when they built a new painting school for the Royal College of

Art in Kensington Gore. To my horror, when I went to see it, they faced east. She was always very professional.

On the day of Churchill's funeral in 1965, I flew to California with them and Kasmin, who was Sheridan's partner in a gallery in Bond Street. I remember someone introducing us as "Mr Kasmin, Mr Lord, Mr Dufferin and Miss Ava – or it might have been Mrs Ava."

She was always a lot of fun. They had many parties in the grand house. I first met Lucian Freud there in 1965. There were all kinds of people there: politicians, artists, bankers, high and low life. I could hear better in those days – so I went to a lot of the parties.

Hanging in their house was my painting, *A Bigger Splash*. It had been bought by Sheridan, when the film director Tony Richardson turned it down: he had had it delivered to his house on Egerton Crescent, kept it for a week and then decided he hated Hollywood.

Lindy knew it wasn't about Hollywood at all. The painting cost them £800. They owned it for many years and when Sheridan died, it went to the Tate.

I remember when Lindy was looking after Sheridan with his fatal illness – she really loved him.

She once told me she wasn't a "shopper", and I believed her. She wasn't really interested in fashion, yet she always dressed well. I assumed she had things made.

It was painting that interested her the most. She had shows in London, Paris and New York, and it was painting that kept me interested in her. She came to see me in Bridlington and watched me make a few pictures. She always had a notebook and jotted down the colours I used.

I remember she kept a diary for appointments and dinners etc, and she was shocked I never did this. I told her my diary was already full for the next twenty years.

She laughed. I miss her.

Lindy, aged 19, in 1960, by Alejo Vidal-Quadras.
She was taught golf by Ben Hogan, the great
American golfer.

A ROUND ON THE SCOTTISH LINKS WITH SHERIDAN AND LINDY

Ferdinand Mount

Ferdinand Mount is a writer. His books include Kiss Myself Goodbye: The Many Lives of Aunt Munca *and* Cold Cream: My Early Life and Other Mistakes. *He was editor of the* Times Literary Supplement *and the Head of Margaret Thatcher's Policy Unit. A friend of Lindy's for sixty years, he was at school and university with Sheridan Dufferin.*

She did it all herself. I've never met anyone else who was quite as self-made as Lindy.

That's an odd thing to say about someone whose mother was a duke's daughter and whose father was a Guinness millionaire and who claimed never to have boiled an egg or done the shopping.

But from the day we met in our late teens until her late seventies, she was always questing and questioning, always eager to learn some new trade or art – painting, dairy farming, property development, golf course design, forestry, stained glass – and to make friends with the best person to teach her.

She was an unnervingly attentive listener – which is another odd thing to say, considering how bossy she was and that she was appallingly deaf for most of her later life. But her curiosity was part of her charm, and even when she put on her delicious daffy look or tossed her frizzy curls and threw her head back in her wicked laugh, she was still soaking it all up.

She was sent off to one of those useless schools that parents like hers deliberately chose for their daughters to prevent them being educated: 'Lawnside' – the very name exhales well-bred ignorance. She persuaded Duncan Grant to teach her to paint, but what she mostly learnt from him were the arts of warmth and friendship.

For quite a while, her paintings bore his muddy imprint, but in the end, though she had other distinguished tutors, she really taught herself, and in recent years her work kept surprising you with its fresher, sharper edge.

Same thing with the cows. When she first started dragging you round the dairy, you couldn't help thinking "Marie Antoinette", but before you knew it, she was a genuine Yoghurt Queen.

I remember best the happy golf tour that she and Sheridan and our friend Ian Dunlop and I took in August 1966, starting at Clandeboye, then across the sea to Stranraer, to stay with Bobby Corbett at Rowallan and play the great Ayrshire links of Turnberry, Troon and Prestwick, then across Scotland to stay with Ian at North Berwick and face the ultimate challenge of Muirfield.

I can still see the two of them walking down the sun-kissed fairways, Sheridan playing at breakneck speed with a swing as fast as a spin-dryer and Lindy dawdling behind and calling out, "Wait for me, Lover," while she rehearsed the slow graceful arc that she had been taught by the immortal Ben Hogan when staying at Palm Beach with her father.

A privileged start, yes, but how many of Hogan's pupils went on to mastermind two formidable golf courses, as she did at Clandeboye?

To think of her as eternally sitting for her old friend David Hockney or lounging by the pool with Mark Boxer is not only to ignore her serious side but to forget what Northern Ireland was like for most of her married life.

The Troubles had not yet broken out when she walked down the aisle with Sheridan in Westminster Abbey. But she stood dauntless through the worst of them, when the Paras were on the streets of Belfast and automatic weapons poked through the battlements of Derry. She made friends with pretty much every Secretary of State and First Minister of whatever party, from Peter Mandelson to Arlene Foster.

She was always looking for ways to restore the cultural life of the Province, from the woodlands to the concert hall. And what she left behind at Clandeboye is only part of the wider influence she radiated throughout Northern Ireland.

In May twenty years ago, she led Peter Mandelson and Julia, my wife, and me on a walk through the woods at Clandeboye, and we came across the Northern Ireland Puppy Trials in full swing. Peter had forgotten to bring a lead for his famous dog Bobby, and I chivalrously offered to lend him my belt.

Spotting the Secretary of State, the ruddy Ulster dog-fanciers chorused with delight, "Good morning, Mr Mandelson, we saw ya on the tullyvision last night," while Peter tried to restrain Bobby from going for the puppies and I was desperately trying to hold my trousers up and Lindy couldn't stop giggling, and I wondered how many private citizens had done more than she had to bring Northern Ireland back together.

Walter Scott, in his epic poem *Rokeby*, laments that, after the Flight of the Earls and the Protestant take-over,

> "…now the stranger's sons enjoy
> the lovely woods of Clandeboy!"

With Lindy gone, there will be new stranger's sons and daughters to walk those lovely woods. But what a lot she has left for them to enjoy.

Van Morrison and Lindy, Clandeboye, 2010.

The Lady and Sir Van

Van Morrison

Sir Van Morrison has been one of the world's leading singers and songwriters for over fifty years. His greatest hits include 'Brown Eyed Girl', 'Moondance' and 'Bright Side of the Road'. A friend of Lindy's for thirty years, he regularly came over to Clandeboye from his home in nearby Cultra to see her – and to rehearse and record in the banqueting hall.

We met in the early nineties at the Aspects Festival in Bangor. I would come a couple of times a year to Clandeboye.

We didn't talk much about music. But we did some performances in the house. There was often a gathering with a few people at Clandeboye. We did some songs. Hannah Rothschild [the writer and daughter of Lord Rothschild] was here singing some back-up. She was pretty good.

Lindy and I were friends at some level. We're both eccentric. She invited me quite a few times to Clandeboye.

She was kind enough to let me use the Banqueting Hall for rehearsal and recordings. We recorded several things there – it's got good acoustics. I like recording in different places. And I had three birthday parties there.

Several times I was at Clandeboye with Lindy and

Ian Adamson, the historian. She loved talking about the historical aspect of this area. He was particularly interested in the early medieval people – the ancient kindred, who were indigenous originally, the Cruthin.

She loved talking about it and was obviously interested in literature and painting too.

I left home very young – 16/17 and basically went on the road. The job involved a lot of travelling. But then I came back to live in Northern Ireland, not far from Clandeboye and Bangor. Lindy and I were going to set up a centre together in Bangor but it didn't really get very far.

Bangor was quite a place when I was young – it was our seaside resort. I spent quite a lot of time in Bangor when I was younger – at the Queen's Hall there, we'd play gigs. There was quite a buzz going on here in the sixties.

You get more fresh air here. You get away from the city environment and come home.

On one occasion, or so Lindy told me cheerfully, Sir Van's band stayed a little too long in the library at Clandeboye and slightly over-indulged at the drinks tray. Lindy awoke to find some slumbering musicians in the library and promptly kicked them out.

Van Morrison continues: There could have been a falling-out over that. I'm not really sure what it was about. She invited a lot of people over for drinks. There was a lot of drink taken. I think she thought we were taking advantage of her drinks cabinet. She could be a bit of a gossip.

Still, though, any minor falling-out was completely healed shortly afterwards. As Sir Van says, "It was a shock when she died."

Painting with Lindy

Catherine Goodman, Emma Tennant, Linda Heathcoat-Amory, Amanda Caledon, Alison Rosse

Catherine Goodman is Artistic Director of the Royal Drawing School in London. She won the Royal Academy Gold Medal in 1987 and the BP Portrait Award at the National Portrait Gallery in 2002. A great friend of Lindy's, she often painted with her in Clandeboye and around the world.

Lindy met Duncan Grant one evening around a bonfire at Charleston, when she was 17.

She loved telling the story of their meeting as a "coming home" and of finding her father figure. Unlike anyone else up until then, he took her talent seriously and showed her how painting could be a way of life. He encouraged her to go to the Slade, where she found her feet as an artist but always stayed in his orbit somehow.

Lindy was an entirely natural painter and had an extraordinary talent. Being very aware of her multiple privileges, she always found it very hard to describe herself as a professional artist but she was one. Painting was her life, her therapy, her companion in deafness and her spiritual and philosophical connection to the world.

When I was staying with her at Clandeboye, there was nothing she liked more than to get us right to the chapel door on a Sunday morning – only to say, hearing the organ playing inside, "Let's skip it and go and find it in nature!" Then revel in the freedom of a morning spent painting by the lake.

She was immensely prolific, consistently competitive and, like all good artists, forever striving for a more complete understanding of her craft.

As Lindy Guinness, she exhibited widely and frequently all her life at the Fine Art Society and Browse & Darby, as well as in New York and Paris.

She was deeply connected through her love of the natural world to the English/Irish Romantic tradition of landscape painting. Jack Yeats, William Blake, William Nicholson, Ivon Hitchens and John Craxton were her touchstones. She was always experimenting with language and medium.

Confidence strangely often eluded her but this didn't constrain a life spent painting to a pulse she knew was there at the heart of nature. It offered her sanity.

Often privately despairing and feeling she'd lost her way, she pushed on with courage late into the night on a few beers, only to be amazed at what appeared the next morning.

***

Lindy the Teacher – Emma Tennant

Lady Emma Tennant is a botanical artist. She and her husband, Toby Tennant, were great friends of Lindy and Sheridan for many years.

Lindy would have made a great teacher.

She gave me priceless advice at exactly the right moment. I was struggling to draw with pencils, getting everything wrong, and rubbing out page after page. Lindy told me to throw away my pencils and use indelible ink instead. It seemed to be impossible advice.

"What happens when I make a mistake?" I asked.

"You'll just have to grow up and get it right first time," she replied robustly.

To my great surprise, I found that, with practice, I could do as she said.

I wouldn't be where I am now as an artist without her incredibly helpful tips and encouragement.

Emma Tennant was spot on, incidentally. In her diary, Lindy wrote in 2019, "I'm a misfit. If I hadn't been born and given all I have, I would be a teacher in a rural town – bossy and impressed by royalty."

***

Lindy the Lioness – Linda Heathcoat-Amory

Linda Heathcoat-Amory, a friend of Lindy's for half a century, is an artist.

Lindy never grew old.

In spite of her deafness, she managed to communicate well, particularly with young people. Her sheer joy and excitement in every single day was infectious and these clever and talented girls and boys lapped it up.

I did too on the very first day we met … nearly fifty years ago. I was shy, silent and awkward and Lindy transformed me. She doled out a helping of confidence, honed my sense of humour and we were away on a lifetime of adventures.

There were cross-dressing wild weekends at Clandeboye, and a lot of competitive tennis and bridge, and Freda round the billiard table. Our hosts excelled at everything, but they made it fun and we all tried harder to win.

The same guests and many, many more then showed up at late-night parties at Holland Villas Road, particularly for Sheridan's birthday in July.

Soon Lindy and I set off for painting trips: Greece, Morocco, India, Italy. Travelling, laughing, competing, working odd hours in remote and squalid places…

These trips were always fraught with practical problems, missing planes, turning up at the wrong hotel, trying to find friends. But we didn't care.

Lindy generally managed to put a show together after two weeks. She loved the secrecy of how she'd put it on and where. And I was just jealous. She was always up at first light and telling me to do the same.

In March 2020, we planned together another party after my exhibition. She adored the planning and encouraged me to invite lots of friends to Holland Villas Road. Just at that planning lunch, I saw a flicker of loneliness cross her brow. That was the last time I saw her.

A few days before she died, she texted me, "I feel safe and as brave as a Lioness."

She was, and I miss her every day.

***

A Friend in Need – Amanda Caledon

The Countess of Caledon lives at Caledon Castle in County Tyrone. Her husband, the Earl of Caledon (referred to as Nicki, below), is Lord Lieutenant of County Armagh.

I did so want to share how outstandingly kind Lindy was to Nicki and me when both of us were at a particularly low ebb.

Lindy touched the lives of everyone whom she met in so many different ways, but also in her own inimitable way: with extraordinary warmth and generosity, candour and charm. It was no different for me.

Arriving in Ireland 15 years ago, rather overwhelmed and with literally no point of reference except my darling husband Nicki, I was so grateful to meet Lindy who scooped me up and instantaneously made me feel as if we had been friends for ever.

She was, as we all know, immensely kind and twinkly, and so at once I was made to feel that I belonged. I felt exceptionally lucky to have come into her orbit; she had the most wicked sense of humour but also the sharpest of minds.

And she never missed a trick ... no matter that she was unable to hear, her startlingly blue eyes caught every detail of everything.

And so it was during the summer of 2017 that, in her typically sweet and sensitive way, sitting next to Nicki at a smart dinner reception, she picked up on his silent pain. That year was our annus horribilis: Nicki had just lost his dear younger sister to a very swift and aggressive cancer, while I was witnessing my mother enduring the final months of a much longer battle with the same disease. There was also other emotional background noise with which we were struggling. We had hit a low spot.

But, having tuned into it, Lindy hit on a solution ... to teach us to paint. In oils. Over a weekend. At Clandeboye.

And what a weekend we had. It was the greatest of fun, and utterly absorbing. She was an enormously gifted teacher and had assiduously prepared our daily lessons: from providing a full set of the essential kit necessary for our painting sessions, to paring down the skills needed to transfer a large rolling landscape onto a small flat board to such brilliant and easily absorbable basics. Nicki and I loved every minute.

With her exuberance and energy, she made the whole process an utter joy, combining detailed knowledge and expertise with infectious spirit and vigour. And just as she had anticipated, we lost ourselves in the moment, freed up from grief as we focused on turning splodges of oil paint into something recognisable. She gave us the gift of art, and a glimpse of its transformational powers.

I shall forever be grateful to Lindy: she was a deep soul, universally generous, inordinately fearless, a consummate hostess, astonishingly thoughtful and incredibly amusing. A light has truly gone out.

PS And Lindy was never one to miss an opportunity. Once the art lessons were over, we were put to use weeding the lawn…

***

Into the Wild West of Ireland – Alison Rosse

The Countess of Rosse is an artist. She and the Earl of Rosse live at Birr Castle, County Offaly.

I first met Lindy when she came to Birr to write something for a magazine in the 1970s when my parents-in-law were still here.

We lived in Iran at that time, and I was going to Afghanistan – as one did in those days! She told me to get a good camera and write something about buzkashi, the national sport. It was a sort of polo but much fiercer and was played with the bladder of a goat. My photos were not a success, as I was much too nervous to get anywhere near it.

After that, we talked about painting. I was amazed by her knowledge and confidence when, one day, staying at Clandeboye, she gave an impromptu lecture on the history of art. It was a wet day and we couldn't go into the garden to paint. There were others there and some of the staff and we listened entranced as she talked for almost an hour without slides.

She was a huge inspiration to me. She showed me the importance of being disciplined, painting for hours on end regularly, and how she fitted it into her busy life.

We went on journeys to the Burren, meeting there to paint the strange lunar landscape. She would paint unstoppably in all weathers, long after I was happy to give up. Once we stayed in a beautiful, empty house belonging to a friend in the centre of the Burren where she showed further talent by cooking a delicious meal.

Inspired by the success of the Burren trips, we went to the Arran Islands. Looking at the scenery on the way, we almost missed the boat, and I remember running down the quay in a great fluster with paintbrushes and bags falling about us.

Travelling with Lindy was always a joy; she was unstoppable at getting where she wanted, whatever obstacles were in the way. On Inishmore, we hired bicycles and explored, and Lindy painted some of her most beautiful small landscapes, looking west over the great cliffs. I too found my inspiration with her.

Recently, I admired her amazing new work on Instagram and I hoped we might repeat some of these small journeys. But it was not to be. I can hear her voice now and regret that I didn't have another chance to be at the receiving end of that amazing force of life.

FUNNY GIRL – AND A CLEVER ONE

Roy Foster

Professor Roy Foster was the Carroll Professor of Irish History at Hertford College, Oxford. He wrote Modern Ireland: 1600–1972 *(1988) and edited* The Oxford History of Ireland *(1989). He is the biographer of W. B. Yeats, Charles Stewart Parnell and Lord Randolph Churchill.*

I first met Lindy in the late 1970s through our joint membership of the British-Irish Association. Its main *raison d'être* was to organise annual conferences held at an Oxford or Cambridge college, where civil servants, politicians and opinion-makers involved in the Northern Ireland imbroglio could meet disputatiously under Chatham House rules – though, given the presence of loose cannons like Conor Cruise O'Brien, these were often spectacularly breached. The BIA continues to flourish today, under the admirable direction of Francesca Kay. Back then its administrator was Marigold Johnson, who managed to be both charming and bossy, and needed to be.

Due to Marigold's cut-glass tones and the membership of people such as Lindy, Thomas Pakenham, Jane Ewart-Biggs and Hugh O'Neill (later Lord Rathcavan), the organisation was christened by Irish quidnuncs "Toffs Against Terrorism".

Lindy was certainly a toff by the most exacting standards, but she was the opposite of toffee-nosed. Meetings in the BIA's poky office, buried deep in a Soho rabbit-warren owned by the Rowntree Trust, were enlivened by her erratic but often on-the-spot suggestions about Northern Irish figures to draw into the conference web, delivered with her characteristic interrogative peals of laughter.

I was struck by her acumen, the way she concealed it, and her highly developed sense of the ridiculous.

But her interest in Northern Ireland was far from light-hearted and she was a serious character. Marriage to Sheridan and the inheritance of Clandeboye conferred a deep commitment which she lived up to, pouring much of her great emotional, imaginative and financial resources into the estate and working to ensure its continuance and relevance to its troubled hinterland. She was determined that it would continue to flourish after her, and built up networks with local charitable organisations to that end.

She also devoted much effort to seeing that the copious archives of the 1st Marquess of Dufferin and Ava should be used to produce a proper biography.

Lord Dufferin was an archetypical late-Victorian grandee who held viceregal posts in Ireland, Canada and India. Clandeboye was full of memorials of his life and times (including a solid gold Buddha with ruby eyes, squatting wisely on Lindy's crowded dressing-table).

At my suggestion, she appointed as biographer the

Eton-based historian Dr Andrew Gailey, whose brilliant and prize-winning *The Lost Imperialist* (2016) placed Dufferin's life in the context of "myth-making in an age of celebrity".

Lindy liked this approach; she knew a lot about myth-making as well as celebrity. Her inimitable, fey glamour, accentuated by the long affliction of deafness, concealed an extremely sharp mind and uncompromisingly intelligent judgement.

What she cared about went deep, shown by her impressive accomplishment as a painter; those wonderfully rich studies of cattle and sunlight at Clandeboye brought together a combination of her great loves.

She was adept at spotting which causes and people were worth adopting and sticking to, and which were time-wasters. Always interested in youth and education, and deeply regretting not having gone to university, late in life she forged links to the enterprising new centre for advanced studies in the humanities founded at Trinity College Dublin, known as the Long Room Hub.

The last time I met her was at a symposium there. We both stayed in Trinity and had breakfast together the next morning; as usual, she made me laugh so much that I missed my mouth with my fork.

When I heard, not long afterwards, that she had died, it was a shock; her liveliness seemed irrepressible.

My mind went back, not to Trinity, but to looking through photograph albums at Clandeboye long ago. They were full of pictures of an owlish Sheridan and ineffably fashionable Lindy in the early 1960s; both looked absurdly young, slightly uncomfortable, orphans of the storm – a very privileged storm, but no less buffeting for that.

Life dealt Lindy an extraordinary hand, which could have been played very differently. She drew on great resources, and put them to good and lasting use. There will be no one quite like her again.

A Beer for Lindy Guinness

Victoria Getty

Lady Getty is a philanthropist, farmer and trustee of the J. Paul Getty Trust. She is the widow of John Paul Getty Jr.

I have myriad memories of our Lindy: a kaleidoscope of scenes at Clandeboye, of feasts at Helen's Tower, her beloved gardens in the spring full of magnolias, rhododendrons, giant echium and bees of course in the Bee Palace [the 1828 bee house in the walled garden, designed by Belfast architect Thomas Jackson]; her prize Holsteins and beautiful Jersey cows and their prizes.

All to a soundtrack of her unforgettable voice full of certainty and wonder, her sparkling blue eyes and freckled, girlish face, full of joy. She was quite simply the most wonderful comet of a person who enriched our lives beyond measure.

One rather charming recent vignette springs to mind of her coming for supper in my flat in Fulham Road – she wanted to try my organic, home-bred beef. I duly prepared a delicious cold fillet, salad etc. I thought I'd thought of everything – but she wanted a beer.

"Oh dear," said I. "Haven't got any."

"There's a pub just there, next to the hospital. Let's go," said she.

So, arm in arm, we took on the traffic and burst into

the Crown and asked for two very cold beers. As we know, her conversation was conducted at high volume – so we were viewed with great curiosity, and almost immediately asked if we were busy and wouldn't we like to join up with these delightful fellows who had fallen under her spell?

"Oh God, this is such fun – can't we stay?" Lindy asked.

But we went home, ate our supper and the steak got a thumbs-up – it was Lindy who had encouraged me to get the Red Poll herd.

We talked about life and farming – rare breeds etc etc.

As she left, she said, "Victoria, you do know, don't you, that if you have a goat, you have a goat problem." Words of wisdom from the Dalai Lama. They ring in my ears on a daily basis.

What a girl. What a brilliant star she was … greatly missed but she continues to be my inspiration.

Cubist Cows by Lindy, 2009.

Champion Cows – and Champion Yoghurt

Mark Logan and Bryan Boggs

Mark Logan is the farm manager at Clandeboye, where he has worked for over thirty years. He and Lindy won many awards for their herd of cows. Lindy said in her diaries, "I always delight in seeing Mark – he is a very dear companion in my life – looks after me and cares so much."

Covid restrictions caused the cancellation of all agricultural shows in 2020. But the Winter Fair decided to host an online event on 10 December and combine it with a People's Champion of the Decade. Photographs of all the breed champions of the last ten years were posted and the public asked to vote for their favourite.

One of our cows, Cookie, was named Jersey Champion and then the vote was opened up again, with the Ayrshire, Holstein, Jersey and Shorthorn Champions competing for the coveted title.

Very sadly, Lady Dufferin died less than two months before – but I know she would have been as delighted as I was when Cookie was declared the overall winner and People's Champion of the Decade. I shared the news with Cookie but she couldn't have cared less – she just continued to eat silage.

The Cookie family continues to grow with the addition of a granddaughter: Christmas Cookie, a very welcome present on Christmas morning, 2020. Cookie provided some happy moments in what for so many reasons had been a very difficult year.

***

The second time I met Lady Dufferin probably set the tone for a working relationship and friendship that was to last almost thirty years. I had come to Clandeboye a couple of months earlier as the new cow man with a promise of the farm manager role if things worked out.

I was doing something with a cow in the paddock below the dairy and, in the distance, I could see Lady Dufferin working her way towards me, driving golf balls as she came.

I had no idea what to expect but we chatted for a while – about what, I have no idea – and then off she went. Later I was to learn she had left the mansion house that day in a foul mood having torn strips off Robbie John, the head woodsman who doubled as butler, for cleaning silver when he should have been out working in the woods.

Apparently I had a very soothing influence and she left me with her mood restored, ready to tackle the rest of the day.

As time passed, we met on occasion and I was fortunate that, in 1991, dairy farming was reasonably profitable and under my management the existing dairy herd responded well and flourished.

Lady Dufferin was always passionate about her cows and I think she enjoyed my enthusiasm for – or perhaps obsession with – them and my desire to create a top-class pedigree herd.

There was an occasion when she mentioned to her brother that she and I hoped to create one of the top pedigree herds in the country. His less than encouraging response seemed to spur her on to becoming even more committed to the idea.

We began a grading-up process with the existing cows in the herd and added a few pedigree cows purchased from local herds. Thirty years later, we still have several families that trace back to those original Clandeboye cows, along with several purchased families from the UK, Ireland and Canada.

Quite early on this journey, Lady Dufferin came back to Clandeboye from London and arrived at the dairy with a story and a question. She had been to dinner with the de Rothschilds of Ascott Farms, who at that time owned the renowned Eranda herd of pedigree Holstein Friesians. During the evening, the conversation turned to the cows and the importing of cattle from Canada.

The questions to me were "Is that really possible?" and "Would you like to?" I just about managed to answer yes and YES.

So, in 1993, 1994 and 1996, I had trips to Canada and purchased four heifers from three families. All three are represented in the current herd although the Rosina line has far outnumbered the Fawns and Marq Is. Over the next few years, the herd gradually improved and we began to take cows out to shows.

Our success was limited at first. When we had a second place with a heifer at the 1999 Royal Ulster Winter Fair, it seemed like a major achievement. Lady Dufferin was on hand not only to enjoy the prize but also to make a sketch of the proceedings. That particular heifer, Jingle, modelled for several portraits.

The year 2000 saw major changes, with renovation of the cow accommodation and plans for a new milking parlour. Following lengthy and intense discussions between Lady Dufferin, John Witchell (the agent) and myself, we decided to go in a completely different direction to the vast majority of dairy farmers, by reducing our cow numbers from 130 to 80 and concentrating on excellence.

Lady Dufferin's attitude to this was pivotal in the decision. Based purely on economics, we should have been milking 200-plus cows.

As often happened, she asked an unexpected question: "Mark do you really want to milk all those cows?"

My answer was that, in an ideal world, I would prefer a smaller number of cows we could treat as individuals and that's what we did. In conjunction with the reduction came the arrival of the first Jersey cows at Clandeboye. It was my idea but Lady D was soon fully on board.

By the time the 2000 Winter Fair came along, we were showing both Holsteins and Jerseys. Our first taste of major success came with the Reserve Champion Jersey at that event.

Through the early 2000s, we had success at many shows with both breeds – notably the 2002 Royal Ulster

Spring Show, where Camomile was Jersey Champion and Reserve Interbreed Champion. I can vividly remember a group of farmers lifting Lady Dufferin over the railings to join in the celebration and the photos.

Clandeboye Champion Willow was our dominant show cow in the late 2000s, winning numerous local and UK awards with Lady Dufferin very often in attendance, cheering us on and always sketching.

Alongside the showing, we also entered the Holstein Northern Ireland herds competition. In 2007, that dream of producing a top-class herd was realised, when Clandeboye Holsteins won the best herd in Northern Ireland. This qualified us for the UK competition, where we saw off fierce competition from English, Scottish and Welsh herds, to be named Holstein UK's Premier Pedigree Herd.

I think, for both me and Lady Dufferin, this was the stand-out achievement. Winning shows is thrilling but to have bred and developed an entire herd to the standard required to win a UK-wide title was certainly beyond my wildest dreams. I think Lady Dufferin really enjoyed sharing the news with her brother!

However, despite our success, with a collapse in milk prices and smaller numbers, the financial viability of the herd was very much in question. Once again, Lady Dufferin proposed a way forward that, in all honesty, John Witchell and I tried to ignore but she persevered and thankfully prevailed. To add value to our product, we began to make yoghurt.

The herd competition win and taking the Supreme Championship at the Royal Ulster Spring Show with

Willow in the same year had proved timely, affording opportunities to promote the newly established Clandeboye Estate Yoghurt. The herd competition even got us a spot on local TV.

As many will know, Clandeboye Estate Yoghurt, the only yoghurt made in Northern Ireland, has gone from strength to strength, supplying not only local shops but all major supermarkets across the island of Ireland.

The last major project Lady Dufferin committed to before her untimely death was the construction of a purpose-built creamery on a greenfield site at Clandeboye to allow the business to grow further and confirming the ongoing commitment to a dairy herd at Clandeboye.

The cows gained a new role in promoting the yoghurt business with lots of photo opportunities. One of these led to Lady Dufferin's first visit to a supermarket, where she was photographed leading a Jersey cow away from the door of a Tesco's store.

On another occasion, we took a cow to Costa Coffee and Lady Dufferin was pictured, coffee in hand, while Cookie licks her lips as the lady from Costa displays the yoghurt.

The Royal Ulster Winter Fair has been a tremendous showcase for our Jersey herd. Between 2010 and 2019, we have had the Jersey Champion on seven occasions. Whilst all have been memorable, the 2012 win with CR Evita, where we also took the Supreme Interbreed title, is probably the highlight and therein lies another story.

In 2011, we took the decision to hold a herd-reduction sale to raise capital to invest in the growing yoghurt business. Lady Dufferin knew I was struggling with selling almost 100 of our cows, including some of the top individuals. So she proposed to buy, from her "painting account", one Holstein and one Jersey.

She enlisted the help of a neighbouring farmer to act on her behalf at the auction which was held in the Pedigree Sales Arena, Moira, and attracted a very large crowd of potential buyers. My pick of animals was duly noted but the Holstein I chose was top price and went off to a new owner.

The Jersey, CR Evita, was purchased by Lady Dufferin, reducing the painting account by 3,000 guineas. Just over a year later, she gave us that amazing win at the Winter Fair. She produced her seventh calf in September 2020 – which to Lady Dufferin's delight was a beautiful heifer calf called Everest Evita.

The current star on the show team is Clandeboye Tequila Cookie, the one declared People's Champion of the Decade in December 2020. An outstanding Jersey and a big character, she has won numerous Championships and All Britain Awards.

Having being named the People's Champion of the Decade at the 2020 virtual Royal Ulster Winter Fair, Clandeboye Tequila Cookie made a triumphant return to the show-ring at the live 2022 event. Having won her class, she then took the Jersey Breed Championship, with the judge saying it was the easiest championship decision he had ever made.

She then overcame the Ayrshire, Holstein and Shorthorn Champions to be named Supreme Interbreed Champion. The judge commented that he didn't know where you would find a better mature Jersey cow anywhere in the world.

Tequila Cookie's daughter Caramel Cookie made her showing debut on the same day. After winning the Jersey heifer in milk class, she defeated the Ayrshire and Holstein heifers to be named Interbreed Champion Milking Heifer and was described by the judge as world-class. A real chip off the old block, or should that be crumb from the original cookie?

For any breeder to win both these interbreed titles on the same day at the Winter Fair is unprecedented. To do it with a mother and daughter is almost unbelievable. Tequila Cookie is now bowing out at the top and retiring from the show-ring. Caramel Cookie can hopefully follow in her mother's footsteps and fly the flag for Clandeboye.

Clandeboye Tequila Cookie also starred in many promotional photos with Lady Dufferin, although, being such a celebrity, it's not always easy to have her concentrate on the job at hand. Getting her to prick her ears and look interested can be problematic. Of course sometimes the photographer had similar problems with Lady D when she hadn't turned her hearing aids on or was choosing not to listen.

Alongside the dairy herd, Clandeboye also keeps a small herd of rare breed Irish Moiled cattle (known as Moilies). Native to Ulster, this ancient breed is naturally polled, and red and white in colour.

Lady Dufferin was keen to have cows, with calves at foot, grazing the park in front of the Mansion House. The native rare breed seemed the perfect choice, although our initial interest came to an abrupt end when we were asked an enormous price for two breeding females.

A year or two later, Lady D met Ian Murray at a shoot and discovered he kept one Irish Moiled cow and had a yearling heifer for sale. She was purchased for a reasonable price and a couple more heifers were added the following year.

We now have around ten cows and visitors to Clandeboye can see them grazing contentedly in the Gymkhana field or wildflower meadow throughout much of the year.

One of Lady Dufferin's last cattle projects was using the Moilies to graze woodland areas. It caused me some difficulties as fences and water supplies to some of the areas were far from ideal but we made it work and will continue the practice as far as practicable.

Lady Dufferin's contribution to Clandeboye Estate has been immense. Her ideas and vision are an inspiration to all of us who live and work here.

I shall be forever grateful for the opportunities she gave me. The support and freedom to create our outstanding herds of Holstein and Jersey cattle and the doors that were opened to me in the pedigree cattle and agricultural communities.

Most of all, I am thankful for the friendship, the morning coffee (usually at lunchtime) in my cottage on a Saturday or Sunday when she wanted a break from painting. There we talked about all manner of things – politics, art, the environment, education, philosophy (she often lost me there), Clandeboye and of course cows.

She is greatly missed. Clandeboye will never be the same again.

**

What a business brain – Brian Boggs

Bryan Boggs has been the Manager of Clandeboye Estate Yoghurt since 1999. Clandeboye Estate Yoghurt is the only yoghurt made in Northern Ireland. In 2008, Lindy dreamt up the idea of using the milk from her award-winning herd of pedigree Holstein and Jersey cows to make yoghurt.

The range is now stocked in all the major supermarket chains and many independent outlets throughout Northern Ireland and beyond. The yoghurts have won many awards, including three stars in the Great Taste Awards, Gold in The Blas na hEireann, and the UK and Irish Quality Food Awards.

It is still so hard to take in that I won't get the chance for any more walks and chats with Lady Dufferin around the estate. She was a remarkable lady and was so good at encouraging and getting the best from us all.

When talking about building our new creamery, she told me all she could do was see talent in people and give them opportunities. The encouragement and confidence I took from all our meetings was amazing.

She was able to make you see you were part of something much bigger and more important than a regular food business – it was quite inspirational. She told me the yoghurt business was to be the "engine" for the estate and help protect its future. She knew how best to motivate and get the best from us all.

The first time I invited the buyers from Aldi to meet us, they had afternoon tea with Lady Dufferin. It helped develop a very close relationship with them. They still talk about their visits and the amazing Lady Dufferin. The fact that she kept saying Lidl instead of Aldi to them – I had to keep nudging her under the table – just added to the experience and made it all the more memorable for them.

Attending the Quality Foods Awards in the Grosvenor House Hotel in London with Lady Dufferin, where we won both the best yoghurt in the UK and the best dairy product, was a very special night. I don't think she could believe we had won and she was the life and soul of the party. From dancing across the floor as we went up to accept the award to her sneaking behind the bar to get some champagne because neither of us liked the cherry cocktails they were serving, it was an experience which will live long in my memory.

All in all, I feel so grateful to have had the chance to learn from and work with such an inspirational person and will be forever grateful for the opportunities she has given me.

A Friend across the Generations

Dora Loewenstein

Princess Dora Loewenstein has known Lindy all her life. She runs an event management company, Dora Loewenstein Associates, and is a trustee of the Clandeboye Estate.

Sadly, I do not remember Lindy when I first met her – but she certainly remembered me! We lived in the same street – Holland Villas Road. I, at the time of our first encounter, was pram-bound.

She used to describe the sight of me being pushed up the street with great delight. I was, according to Lindy, elegantly got up in all manner of bonnets and outer wear covered by starched linens and cosy blankets.

I sat up, or was propped up, as much as one could be in those old-fashioned perambulators, peering out at the world passing by. What amused her the most was the smart coronet on the side of the pram!

Later, as I grew, she saw me in matching hats, coats and gloves – getting in trouble with nanny as I dragged my hands, dirtying my gloves, along all the low walls of the houses on Holland Villas Road en route to Holland Park.

I wish I had been aware of Lindy at that time! I am sure she would have encouraged me more in my endeavours to engage in the rough and tumble of what Holland Park had to offer.

At that time, my brother Rudolf has fond memories of Lindy and Sheridan coming to our house up the road – saying, always, that they were both so unbelievably friendly to him, which as we all know was rare as oftentimes friends of our parents' generation could dismiss the younger generation out of hand.

My proper adult reunion with Lindy came much later, when I was about twenty. We were both fortunate enough to be hosted frequently by Ingrid and Paul Channon (later Kelvedon) on the island of Mustique. Here we cemented a friendship which was to grow year by year, and which I valued beyond all else. I am eternally grateful to the entire Channon family for this and all the many other kindnesses and opportunities their generosity afforded me.

I am not going to explain my friendship with Lindy or to trace it historically as it would be indulgent of me and boring for others. I would, however, like to concentrate on one particular attribute which I always observed and which I believe touched the lives of so many, and that was her remarkable ability to get on with, engage with and entrance children. It is an attribute that does not come naturally to everyone and least of all to those who have not had children, and in this alone there is a certain pathos.

Lindy had a side to her character which was enchantingly childlike. Perhaps because she had not had the easiest of upbringings herself, but more importantly the avid curiosity that she possessed throughout her life was akin to that of a young child. Her imagination felt as if it could explode at all times, and her hunger to discover and understand new things, right up until the end, was palpable. I think children recognised this in her, and her in them.

I remember one time in particular, when she came to stay with us in Gloucestershire, when my son, Aliotto, had some science homework – he was about seven years old. The homework was a study about light and how it fell, and how shadows were created dependent on the direction of light.

WELL … can you imagine the joy for Lindy?! She totally refuted what and how the teacher was presenting the study, and in a trice we were plunged into darkness. Torches, candles and objects placed all around the kitchen. She became so involved that she said to an enthusiastic, if a little startled, Aliotto, that she would come into school with him and explain the proper theory of light and shadow! I think he was a little relieved when this did not come to pass.

My children were always captivated by Lindy, as I know were so many. The tributes of those who have written since Lindy died have mentioned the activities and adventures that she produced for children visiting her at Clandeboye. Everything from dry-stone walling; making fires; camping; cooking on campfires; the study of plants and trees; painting classes and of course the tour around the milking parlour with Mark. The whole experience was marvelled at by the children but also I believe much enjoyed by Lindy.

There was another element to her rapport with

children, which went deeper. I believe that, like in all things, Lindy wanted to understand how people worked. How they develop and grow, what motivated them and how they interacted with the world around them, most particularly with nature.

When she spotted bright, interested children, then what better thrill was there but to study them and work out what made them tick? This she did, not in a patronising, didactic way, but in a genuine way to help her own understanding of life and the universe which she endlessly questioned and wanted to work out.

I think the innocence and enthusiasm of children excited her, and in turn she felt she could really give to them in a way others could not. I think she saw this as part of the journey of life.

To me the great sadness was that she never had the opportunity to have children herself. I am sure she discussed that with many people.

We did speak of it a bit, and she said to me that she felt she would have been bad at being a mother – that she could not have borne the massive burden of responsibility and worry that comes with the parental remit! I disagreed with her on that point as I think she would have been an incredible mother.

I do understand though, that what she did give to children, she did with a huge sense of generosity and freedom, but at the end of the day she could re-assign them to their parents – usually exhausted! The relationship then was nothing but positive. Certainly, the children that I know who were close to her, whether mine, or those of close friends, all adored her and all had their unique relationship with her – which is an enormous accomplishment in itself.

I am not sure how many godchildren Lindy had, but I imagine it was a lot [43!]. But whether you were one or not, I think she treated all children as if they were her godchildren. The Pied Piper comes to mind often.

I will end with one small vignette of Lindy taking my son and his cousin Ollie on a painting expedition in Mustique. The plan was made some days ahead and Lindy turned up for the assignation, with paper, paints, her shorts (the very same that she might wear walking in Clandeboye, practising golf swings in Holland Park or around the farm at Clandeboye) and a baseball cap. The boys with hats, shorts and flip flops.

Off they sped in a Mule with no particular destination in sight. They ended up walking down a precipitous cliff to end up on the seafront with waves pounding a rocky shore, with nothing but trees and bushes behind them.

Here they were to do pencil sketches of the rocks on the shore. They each settled down to begin, whereupon a wave came along and swept over Lindy – soaking her completely. Immediately the boys thought that would be "trip over".

Of course not. Lindy immediately stripped off all her clothes to her underwear and carried on painting – totally unperturbed. The two boys, aged thirteen and fifteen, blushed to their roots, not knowing where to look, and tried their best to continue drawing. They certainly never forgot that trip. Perhaps not for the artwork but they came back most definitely bonded more to Lindy than when they left.

How lucky were we all to have been blessed by her friendship and I am so glad that my children also benefited so richly from their own individual relationships with her. She was a unique spirit and one that will be sorely missed.

Whoever she touched, whether young or old, was enriched by her – and that has to be the biggest legacy of all.

MUSIC IN THE COURTYARD

Barry Douglas

Born in Belfast, Barry Douglas is one of our greatest pianists. The founder of Camerata Ireland, the all-Ireland chamber orchestra, he is artistic director of the Clandeboye Festival. He won the gold medal at the 1986 International Tchaikovsky Competition.

As an 18-year-old, I played clarinet in the Belfast Youth Orchestra at a concert in Clandeboye. Everyone had enjoyed a post-concert refreshment.

Lindy knew I was also a pianist. Suddenly out of the blue, she encouraged me spontaneously to play a solo piece to the audience – everyone walked back to the Banqueting Hall from the house to listen.

That was Lindy – encouraging young people; helping them in their first steps.

During our Clandeboye Festival every August, I would walk into Dendron Lodge for a cup of tea. Lindy would be there chatting with the students, encouraging them to work hard and enjoy life.

That was Lindy.

Since I first met her, she encouraged me. She spurred me on. When I suggested in 2000 that it would be fantastic to create a music festival at Clandeboye, modelled on the Marlboro Music Festival in Vermont, she jumped at the idea and understood immediately the value to audiences and students alike.

I founded Camerata Ireland in 1999 – the only all-Ireland orchestra – as a response to the Ireland peace process. Our musicians are from every part of the island. I believe that we artists have a responsibility to comment on, cajole and applaud society. The festival was an obvious continuation of the orchestra. Lindy understood that very well.

We wanted to break down barriers. Audiences, young students and musicians could be together – no "them and us". Soloists and students could chat with the audience and there was a sense of family and friendship.

The festival celebrated its 20th anniversary in August 2021, and excitement and pride at this wonderful collaboration with the estate and Lindy was tinged with sadness that she has left the scene.

From tea parties at Clandeboye for the students every year, to her support of young artists at her home in London, Lindy remained totally engaged and full of ideas. She challenged me and encouraged a feeling of flexibility, creativity and imagination.

Some of my most vivid memories come from the closing gala concert/banquet every festival. She would whisper a beckoning to me to walk around and chat. She had time for everyone and was a huge help to the festival in creating, maintaining and developing new partnerships and friendships with audiences and sponsors.

I will miss her very much. Our Festival/Camerata Ireland office is at the Courtyard at Clandeboye. Her spirit lives on and shines intensely.

Following a recent recording by Camerata in Clandeboye with three talented young musicians, I made a few comments about Lindy to the orchestra. As the musicians ambled into the Courtyard, a glorious double rainbow presented itself. Lindy was looking down. We love you.

The View from Stormont

Arlene Foster

Arlene Foster was First Minister of Northern Ireland, 2016–2017 and 2020–2021. She was Leader of the Democratic Unionist Party, 2015–2021. She was the first woman to hold either position.

I first got to know Lindy Dufferin when she was launching her yoghurt business. I was the Economy Minister at the time and Clandeboye was getting some help from our regional business development agency, Invest NI.

I went out on a site visit to see the factory and Lindy's "girls" – i.e. the cows – and I knew straightaway that this was someone who I would get on with. She was keen on that visit to show me her chequebook as she wanted to show me how much she was spending on shampoo for the cows!!

When I next visited, it was for afternoon tea and she met me at the front door and took me up through all the memorabilia from the 1st Marquess, who obviously lived a fascinating life. The evocative Asian feel was then further enhanced when she introduced me to her tent, which she had erected in one of her rooms – not what you expect of one of the grand houses of Ulster!

Lindy was always concerned about what would happen to her beloved Clandeboye after she left and I, like many others, was engaged in conversations about that. She loved Clandeboye and indeed Northern Ireland and wanted Clandeboye to speak to her love of the place long after she was gone. Her legacy and that of her late husband were something that punctured all of our latter conversations.

She also found time to indulge my huge interest in her early life – goodness, it all sounded so glamorous – parties at Holland Park, debutantes' balls in the fifties. She recounted some great stories over a "few beers".

Her love for art and music was enormous. Her patronage of Camerata Ireland was, I think, something she was very proud of and she so enjoyed meeting the talented young people.

My husband Brian and I loved hearing about her travel and all her exploits and how she would find a space to paint, no matter where she was. Cows always seem to pop up – she recounted how she was painting them in Transylvania on a remote hillside. She and Brian struck it off – she was a tremendous flirt!

Her last email to me was in June 2020 – four months before she died. She wrote to me about the Forest School at Clandeboye. Could I connect someone from the Forest School with people who could help him develop it? She wanted young people from wherever they came to have the chance to explore woodlands and nature. She finished with these words:

"Don't forget I'm expecting you here for a walk as soon as you are both allowed to meet people. Do put me high on your list. I would love to see you both xx Lindy."

I didn't get to see her due to Covid and then her illness.

But I am sure that her legacy will be felt in many ways through Clandeboye, her paintings and her promotion of music and the arts wherever she went.

Lindy's picture of the Library,
Clandeboye, 2020, the year of her death.

A Packed Weekend

Christopher Sykes

Christopher Sykes is a photographer and writer.
He is the author of Hockney: the Biography. *He*
photographed Clandeboye in Great Houses of Ireland,
written by Hugh Montgomery-Massingberd.

I first met Lindy at the Kasmin Gallery in 1965. My mother, who collected younger people, had befriended her and her husband, Sheridan, the co-owner of the gallery.

There was a party there for the opening of some show. I was sixteen and a little green, and felt a bit shy amongst these incredibly glamorous people. But Sheridan and Lindy immediately made me feel welcome, treating me as an equal, not an awkward schoolboy. I fell totally under the spell of Lindy's huge, embracing, smile.

Later that night, after all the other guests had left, my mother and I stayed behind to dance the Twist. This was my first experience of Lindy's love of dancing. I remember laughing with her as we invented our own new dances, one of which was the Sweep, where we pretended to sweep the floor with invisible brooms. I have rarely laughed so much in my life.

This was the beginning of a lifetime's friendship, starting with Sheridan and Lindy being my parents' friends, and then mine too. They were fun to be around, because they had an infectious joy for life and for each other, and their parties in their Holland Park house were legendary, the epitome of the mix of artists, rock stars and aristos for which the sixties became famous.

Lindy and Sheridan were such a partnership that it was hard to mention one without the other, let alone come to terms with there only being one of them, which is what happened when Sheridan tragically died from AIDS at the age of 49.

This brought out two sides of Lindy that were to see her through the next part of her life – her courage and her determination. Since her marriage to Sheridan, a large part of her life had been spent at his family estate, Clandeboye, east of Belfast, a period in which Northern Ireland was being torn apart by the Troubles.

When Sheridan died, in 1988, the country was still in the throes of what amounted to a Civil War, with shootings and bombings taking place on a regular basis.

It would have been only too easy and quite understandable for her to come to the decision that, without him at her side, it was too much to take on.

But giving up was not in Lindy's nature, and she took the brave decision to carry on alone. During the next thirty years, she showed herself to be a formidable chatelaine of this beautiful estate, teaching herself about farming and forestry, creating a quite extraordinary woodland garden, making a highly successful golf course, opening an art gallery, and eventually building up a top-class herd of dairy cows from which she developed her own brand of Clandeboye Estate Yoghurt, of which she was inordinately proud.

Just as she had done in Holland Villas Road, Lindy also turned Clandeboye into a haven of comfort and entertainment, though one needed to be fit to survive a weekend, as every moment was organised, and there was no room for stragglers.

A typical day in the summer would begin with a huge cooked breakfast in the dining room, at which Lindy would give her orders for the day, which might start with a tour of the woodlands followed by a visit to look at her beloved cows.

Then there might be the long trek to Helen's Tower, where one would find Lindy's butler, the faithful and long-suffering Robbie John, standing by a beautifully laid table, ready to hand out much-needed drinks to the walkers. A long lunch would be followed not by a siesta – and woe betide anyone who dared to suggest such a thing – but by another expedition; perhaps a tour of the woodland garden.

When the hardy guests did finally arrive back at the house, they would be rewarded with a fantastic tea laid out in the drawing room, where conversation continued to flow until, finally, they were allowed upstairs to collapse exhausted onto their beds.

That was only a prelude, however, to the evening's activities, beginning with cocktails in the library, then a long dinner in the dining room, at which seconds were always offered, followed by coffee in the museum, games of Freda, dancing, and a return to the library for more drinks. Throughout all this, Lindy never flagged and was invariably the last man standing.

For many years, during the winter months, there

were shooting parties at Clandeboye, a hangover from Sheridan's days, which Lindy carried on with. Naturally she was a crack shot, and her charm and expertise guaranteed that she was invited everywhere.

In the end, however, all the shooting had a debilitating effect on her hearing, and she gradually became very seriously deaf. She dealt with this devastating disability with extraordinary courage, refusing to give in to it, learning to lip-read, and carrying on her life as if there was nothing wrong with her, working as normal in the day, and attending gallery openings, dinners and parties in the evenings as she had always done. This never ceased to amaze me.

She also threw herself into her painting. She had always been a keen artist, ever since I first met her in the 1960s. But, as time passed and her deafness progressed, she devoted more and more hours to it, and got better and better, latterly posting daily paintings of the life and landscape of Clandeboye on Instagram.

I think she took a lot of inspiration from her old friend David Hockney, who she used to visit from time to time at his house in Bridlington.

I remember her saying to me, while on one of these trips, "It's the most extraordinary thing, but I was looking out of my bedroom window at the view of rooftops and streets and houses, just so ordinary and really quite ugly, and yet David, when painting this as a subject, manages to imbue the view with magic."

There was certainly magic in the paintings she was doing in her last months.

Like many others, I find it hard to grasp that Lindy

is no longer with us, that our lives will no longer be lit up by that huge smile, those dazzlingly bright eyes, and the waves of affection that came off her. One thing for certain is that wherever she may now be, she will be the brightest light.

My Magic Man

Brian Moorhead

*Brian Moorhead has worked at Clandeboye for
14 years.*

For many years when I awakened in the morning, I
said to my wife, Carol, "Guess what I dreamt again
last night!"

She knew exactly what I was going to say. I dreamt I
was in a big house with so many rooms I could barely
count them!

I had spent most of my life working happily in printing,
until the firm I worked for was bought out. Everything
changed. After almost a year of giving it my best, I told
Carol I wanted to do something new.

A couple of hours later, a friend called Deborah was
telling us that her daughter Victoria, who was managing
the house at Clandeboye, was looking for somebody to
assist her. I became interested, went to Clandeboye to
see what it was like and felt completely at home. I had
no doubt that this was where I was meant to be.

When I began in Clandeboye, 14 years ago, Lady
Dufferin was at her home in London. Having never met
her, I didn't even know what she looked like! I imagined
somebody like the late Queen Mother in floaty clothes,
waving her hand.

I couldn't have been more wrong. Lady Dufferin

arrived home from London, bouncing in through the library door, and greeted me warmly and appreciatively, bursting with energy as usual.

Working in Clandeboye with Lady Dufferin was always unpredictable (in a good way!). One minute, you would be on your hands and knees with her, looking under every possible piece of furniture for her hearing aid or glasses, which she very frequently mislaid.

The next minute, you would be in the dining room, attending to a dinner party with people such as Christian Louboutin or Kirstie Allsop. On one occasion, I had the pleasure of presenting the late Bamber Gascoigne with his first course and couldn't resist saying "That's your starter for 10!"

"That's my bonus!" he quipped.

It was a great pleasure to meet so many wonderful guests. Lady Dufferin would always introduce each of us on the Clandeboye team by name and tell her guests how wonderful we were!

I always found each guest to be friendly and appreciative, whether they were billionaires, titled or simply ordinary people. Lady Dufferin always seemed to attract people who were inspiring and interesting.

One of the things Lady Dufferin frequently liked to do was change things in the house. She wouldn't hesitate to take one end of a sofa or other piece of furniture or a rug, while I or somebody else would take the other end, and move it to another part of the house. Frequently she decided she preferred it where it had been and we would move it back to its original place!

She would ask your opinion about things, listen

to ideas and if you thought of a better way of doing something, she would run with it gladly. She made great efforts to ensure attention was paid to detail. As I get great pleasure in ensuring that details and order are applied, it was a pleasure to be part of her life.

She was, of course, very funny and frequently used pet names, which came randomly to her, when chatting. Sometimes she would enter a room and call out "Where's my magic man?" (Presumably because I made things appear rather than disappear!)

Lady Dufferin always had a desire to share what she had and would encourage me to explore the grounds along with my wife.

Generosity was one of her strongest attributes. It was a highlight of Christmas to receive a card from her with a personal note of appreciation. She sat in the library for hours each Christmas, writing hundreds of cards, each with a personal message.

She gave me many gifts over the years. I especially treasure a case she brought me from Morocco for my art materials. Like Lady Dufferin, I am a painter. On several occasions, she gifted me canvases and other materials from her studio. It was a privilege after she died to prepare the packing of over 100 of her paintings for a posthumous exhibition in England.

One of my most special memories is receiving an invitation to the chapel service at Clandeboye when the windows she designed were dedicated. Her talk revealed an incredible depth of knowledge, wisdom and understanding. Even though she is gone, her influence continues in so many ways.

I could write endlessly about the great times I have experienced at Clandeboye and what an inspiring person Lady Dufferin was. Memories of her conjure up words like kind, generous, sincere, thoughtful, discerning, witty and loving.

Lady Dufferin had a very different relationship with each person she knew, personalising her conversations to make each person feel special. Not only was she incredibly unique – she made each person she knew feel unique, too.

THE ART OF DIGGER-GARDENING

Fergus Thompson

Fergus Thompson has been the head gardener at Clandeboye since 1998. Lindy and Fergus had a tremendous friendship, with Lindy learning huge amounts about gardening from him. In her diary in August 2019, she wrote, "Fergus taught me about seeds – of cowslips and vetch and clover. An utter delight."

Surprising though it may seem, my acquaintance with Clandeboye pre-dates that of Lady Dufferin by some eight or nine years – but I was just a child visiting one or other of two sets of uncles and aunts and associated cousins, while Lady Dufferin came in 1964 as a worldly wise young lady and bride to take over as the latest member of the Guinness clan to preside as lady of the big house.

My very first memory of Clandeboye was when I came on a walk with my dad and elder brother from a farm in Ballasallagh, which marches with the estate, to see three lakes.

First the small reservoir in what is now the Blackwood Golf Club. Then the Tower Lake with its causeway separating the two parts. And then on, further through woodland and open farmland, to see the "big Clandeboye lake" with its wildfowl and swans and many strange and unfamiliar plants, which were all mesmerising to me!

I can still recall the little collection I had: orchid, ragged-robin, bogbean and bulrush (actually reedmace).

If it had been spring, I'd have no doubt had marsh marigold and cuckoo flower (kingcup and lady's smock) but, regardless, the whole experience was a huge eye-opener to me and maybe even sparked my lifelong interest in plants.

Fast forward thirty-five years or so and imagine my joy at securing the job of head gardener for the Clandeboye Estate and actually getting to deal with Lady Dufferin on a day-to-day basis, instead of having a fleeting glimpse of her or, as often was the case in my youth, when playing with my cousins (the Coulters and McMillans) of trying to avoid both Lord and Lady Dufferin.

It was clear to me from the start in 1998 that Lady Dufferin was a very passionate person with a deep interest in her gardens. This probably started in the mid-60s when she and Sheridan made strides to enhance the collection by the inclusion of an arboretum adjacent to the pinetum established over 100 years earlier.

Somewhere between then and Lord Dufferin's untimely death in 1988, I feel that Lindy's interests lay elsewhere, probably in the art world, mixing with high society, visiting exotic places and dabbling in exotic religions, philosophies and cultures. Certainly her knowledge and abilities as an artist were greatly enhanced through the period.

Before Lord Dufferin died, he repeatedly told her, "After I'm gone, Lindy, don't be making any more gardens." The advice clearly had the opposite effect.

Lady Dufferin once again turned her attention to the gardens. Definitely not flower borders or municipal bedding, however, rather what she envisaged was woodland gardens; more woodland proper, and more care and attention devoted to them.

She decided to carve a memorial garden for her beloved Sheridan out of mature deciduous woodland to the east of Brenda's Garden (started two generations earlier in the twenties and thirties by Lady Brenda).

So, many over-mature beech, ash, sycamore and copious amounts of cherry, laurel and rhododendron ponticum – invasive understorey put in during Victorian times as cover for game – were filled and ripped out, leaving space for many fine shrubs and exotic trees.

It was during the making of Sheridan's garden that Lady Dufferin became a devotee of "digger gardening", though this was in no small measure due to the compliance and versatility of her two stalwart diggermen, Messrs Robin Wilson and James Douglas.

The main species represented in this new garden were rhododendrons, magnolias and maples but also repetitions of plants successful elsewhere in the gardens, as well as many genera new to Clandeboye altogether.

In the former repetition category, such species as Parrotia persica or Cercidiphyllum japonicum, known as the katsura or toffee tree – both wonderful for the autumnal tints. The latter category includes unusual trees and shrubs often collected in the world by personal friends of Lady Dufferin, such as Thomas Pakenham e.g. Betula szechuanica, a beautiful Chinese birch with rich purple exfoliating bark, Deutzia and hydrangea species.

Clandeboye Tequila Cookie, the People's Champion of the Decade at the Royal Ulster Winter Fair, December 2020. In 2022, she won the Jersey Breed Championship. The judge said it was the easiest championship decision he'd ever made.

bist Cows:
ptych by
dy.

"I'm the most famous disposable artist in the world": Lindy paints a picture for the Clandeboye yoghurt labels, 2008.

Dairy Queen: Lindy celebrates supplying milk to Costa Coffee at the branch in Holywood, Belfast, 2012. The cow, Newmoor Sultan Cookie, mother of the champion Tequila Cookie, is the foundation cow for the Clandeboye Cookie family.

"Fergus taught me about seeds – of cowslips and vetch and clover. An utter delight." Lindy with Fergus Thompson, her head gardener.

Lindy, Peter Mandelson, Secretary of State for Northern Ireland, and the writer Ferdinand Mount on top of Helen's Tower, 2000.

Bobby, Peter Mandelson, Lindy, Ava. The 2000 Northern Ireland Puppy Trials were being held in the Clandeboye woods. Mandelson borrowed Ferdinand Mount's belt as a lead for Bobby to keep him from the puppies.

Below: The Lady and Sir Van: with Van Morrison in the library, 2012.

R: Van Morrison returns to Clandeboye after Lindy's death, 2022.

The Hall at Clandeboye.
Harold Nicolson, the 1st
Marquess's nephew, wrote
in *Helen's Tower* (1937),
"The steps which led
down to the front door
were flanked by a double
row of curling stones from
Scotland and from Can-
ada [where Dufferin had
been Governor-General]."

Nicolson added, "The
wall had been covered
with wire netting on
which were affixed dirks,
daggers, cutlasses, pistols,
lances, curling brooms
and a collection of those
neat little fly-whisks with
which the acolytes dust
the high altar of St Peter's
at Rome. Above the wide,
baronial fireplace hung a
portrait of Lord Dufferin
at the age of 23."

"An exceptional Irishman." The 1st Marquess of Dufferin and Ava (1826–1902), Viceroy of India, Governor General of Canada, British Ambassador to France, Russia and the Ottoman Empire. *Vanity Fair* cartoon by Alfred Thompson, 1870.

ROME	Revel and Hilary Manners	Friday 3 30 PM	Sunday. 7.30 PM
CANADA			
INDIA	Lady Dufferin	Thursday 5 30 PM	Wednesday. 11 30 AM
K LEAGH			
FRANCE			
PARIS	Miranda Clow	Friday 3 30 PM	Monday. 11 30 AM
ITALY			Monday 11 30 AM
RUSSIA	Lady Armstrong	Friday 3 30 PM	Sunday - 7 30 PM
ST. PBURG			
WALMER	Oliver & Elaine Robertson	Late Friday night	Sunday 7 30 PM
OTTAWA			
MUTTRA	Eugenia & Julian Sands	Friday 11 30 AM	Tuesday. 7 30 PM
SIMLA			
S LEIDY			
NURSERY	Baby Ruth & Nanny Jackie	Friday 11 30 AM	Tuesday 7 30 PM
A BOURNE			
SYDNEY			

A weekend house party, 1999. The bedrooms are named after the 1st Marquess's diplomatic postings and treasured local places. Members of Lindy's family are staying.

"One of the pleasantest rooms on earth," said Harold Nicolson – the library at Clandeboye. The picture over the fireplace is of the playwright Richard Brinsley Sheridan, ancestor of Sheridan Dufferin. Statues of Greek gods with gilt labels circle the room. Over the Sheridan portrait there's the single Greek word, "Chaos".

"Helen's Tower, here I stand, dominant over sea and land" – Tennyson. Helen's Tower was built by the 1st Marquess in 1861 in honour of his mother, Helen Sheridan, granddaughter of Sheridan the playwright. Sheridan Dufferin took his name from these ancestors.

Dancing Queen:
Ömer Koç's
photo of Lindy at
the Istanbul
Biennial, 2019.

In Memoriam:
with the Sheridan
Windows she
designed in
memory of
Sheridan for
Clandeboye
Chapel, 2019.

'The Ancestors': Lindy's picture of Dufferin portraits at Clandeboye, in the 2020 C
lockdown. During lockdown, between March and September 2020 (weeks before
death on October 26), she painted 162 canvases.

Clandeboye: the Music
Room by Lindy, 2010.

Last self-portrait, 2020.

Patrick Forde brought back Quercus semecarpifolia, the Afghan holly oak, Pinus armandii and Pinus wallichiana, the delightful Asian Pines.

Still others have been added to increase the diversity of the collection and test the bounds of what can be grown in the heavy, slightly acidic soil of Clandeboye.

Here we can include such rarities as the Japanese umbrella pine, Sassafras albidum from eastern USA, Japanese bitter orange and the rubber-producing Chinese Gutta-percha tree.

In addition, Sheridan's garden includes "the Dell" – two small quarry holes where stone was quarried during the famine years of the 1840s to build the walls of the estate. These dells both contain a small, interconnected pond and around were intensely planted with primulas, irises and ferns closest to the water and azaleas, maples, dogwoods and rhododendrons further up. Two towering oaks retained during the initial development dominate the whole, growing on top of the shaley rock that was left when quarrying was discontinued.

Because of the intensity of planting and the passage of time – thirty-three years – the Dell is now full to overflowing – not with water, but plants – and while in the late nineties it was a nightmare job keeping on top of the weeds, by 2015 they were far less of a problem. Rather it was a case of pruning and cutting back to keep as many plants as possible thriving and looking their best.

Over the years, Lady Dufferin and I built up a great relationship in a joint effort to improve and enhance the gardens. We discussed things at length and frequently had hefty debates about how to proceed. Often we would have to sleep on a decision and resume negotiations the following day or sometimes the next time Lindy returned to Clandeboye from London.

Occasionally I would propose a piecemeal approach to a difficult dilemma, which would alleviate the problem in the short term, but invariably LD would prevail.

Two examples come to mind. First, the castellated beech hedge. For quite a considerable time, Lady Dufferin felt this hedge was artistically inappropriate and that it disturbed the view out from the Chapel Walk, south over the parkland to the distant woods. Initially I suggested cutting the long, lower sections much lower (down to two feet) but leaving the pillars intact.

I knew that the sections would grow back in two to four years if we found the arrangement unsuccessful.

Little did I think that, after only one year, LD would make the unilateral decision that "No, this halfway house doesn't help. I need to see out into the landscape and, besides, how are you going to get rid of that wretched ground elder unless we pull the whole damned lot out? Get me Robin (Wilson the digger man) on your phone, Fergus."

And the rest is history.

A week later and the magnificent beech hedge was away, along with huge quantities of ground elder and wild garlic (ramsons).

So, at one fell swoop, Lady Dufferin could see out across the landscape to distant Sir John's Wood, several rhododendrons and Camellias got a new lease of life because the beeches were gone and not sucking up huge quantities of their precious water every summer AND two pernicious weeds were greatly diminished, though impossible to eradicate completely. I'd never have been that bold!

Secondly, the avenue of red flowered horse chestnuts. These were planted by Lady Maureen and lined both sides of the main drive, entering the estate from the old post office gate.

Again LD found them "a dark and dismal tunnel blocking the view to the young oak woods beyond and spoiling the lawns either side every autumn."

I suggested removing every other tree on each side to placate those residents wishing to keep the trees and at the same time making the overall effect much less tunnel-like. I said, "We can always decide to take up more chestnuts but it's a hard job putting them back, LD, if we decide we don't like it. Let's sleep on that one."

Next day, that decision was made and my trusty gardener Aaron and I duly commenced the task, getting three trees safely felled, with all the brush removed, that same day.

The following morning, Lady Dufferin arrived just as we finished our tea and said, "I've looked at your work last night and am now quite sure we need to take out the lot – no more about it." And I heard Aaron say, half under his breath, "Final decision."

Defeated once again, I said, "I'll speak to Robin, Lady Dufferin", meaning that I'd order the digger to dig out stumps, level the lawns and leave no trace of Lady Maureen's chestnuts.

Then there was the case of the ornamental wrought iron oval gate as one entered the Conservatory Garden from the big house.

The sound of this gate banging was often a warning sign of the imminent arrival of her ladyship on the scene! Whilst the gate itself is very fine, LD disliked the fact that when Lady Maureen had it put in, the old wall was partially demolished and the surround redone with new, 1938-vintage brick. We talked long about how to mask "this hideous brick" and eventually settled on the idea of boxwood pillars clipped to shape to disguise the offending brick.

This we duly did and though it took a number of years to grow up and hide everything, today the oval gate with box around is rather fine.

One final example of our trials and tribulations relates to the Thujopsis dolabrata tree at the chapel. This fine old specimen dating from 1900 was deemed to be blocking the long view of the chapel as one approached from the south side.

Lady Dufferin contended that "the artwork and frescoes around the doorway were far more important than that old conifer."

I countered that "This is a sacred tree in Japan and very appropriate that the 1st Marquess in the last years of his life should have deemed it appropriate to plant one here."

I even alluded to LD's own interest in Buddhism and suggested that maybe she would consider crown-lifting the tree (cutting off all the low branches) to the height of the bottom of the chapel roof.

This met with faint approval and I hurriedly got on with the task in hand before any change in mind or policy. The removal of those lower branches opened up a view of the facade of the chapel and subsequently Lady Dufferin designed and commissioned five new stained glass windows for that same side of the chapel. And a mighty fine addition they are too!

After they were placed, LD again started to mention the Thujopsis tree and I felt that its stay of execution was coming to an end. The sad irony is that it was dear Lady Dufferin who was nearing the end of her remarkable life, while the condemned tree has an indefinite reprieve!

Lady Dufferin had a high regard for trees of all kinds but above all she liked oaks. Obviously the grand old parkland oaks which we estimate at around 280 to 320 years of age and over 20 feet in circumference at chest height gained considerable prestige for her and the estate but equally important in her eyes were the bundle of 18-inch to two-feet whips she placed with great precision and equal joy, to fill a small gap in a plantation that had recently lost a few big trees through filling or windblow.

And, better still, these whips were grown on the estate by Pascal McCaughan and his CVNI team, often from seed collected right here in the estate.

The weeping beech, just beyond the tennis court, was another of her favourites. This she called "my Cathedral Tree" and very apt the title is. When one enters in through the canopy towards the trunk, the whole structure is a wonderful labyrinth of interconnected branches, welded together repeatedly and rooted in where they meet the ground. Many of the most heavily shaded branches end in great knobbly gargoyle- or monster-like shapes. An absolute paradise for a young or inquisitive mind!

Another favourite was a monster ash down close to the big lake. This tree died in about 2009 but, despite Barry Garvan having his eye on it as a perfect source of top-quality firewood, LD would not allow it to be felled because "It has such wonderful shapes and character."

Instead she had her mobile painting hut parked under the tree and painted many pictures of the lake and surrounding landscape from the spot. This continued for a number of years on and off until the tree shed more and more rotten branches and was eventually deemed "too dangerous" and had to be felled.

Since her London house was close to Kew Gardens, LD spent many hours visiting each year. She brought back several ideas from Kew to be adopted here in Clandeboye and the relationship really blossomed for a number of years in the early 2000s with Kew sending over not only batches of students for long weekend work parties but also top scientific, horticultural and arboricultural staff members to give talks, take masterclasses and disseminate advice to ourselves and likeminded folk from around Northern Ireland.

Of these, for me at least, the most influential were Tony Kirkham, John Lonsdale and Nigel Taylor and they also facilitated reciprocal trips to Kew's sister garden at Wakehurst Place in Sussex. All this accumulation of knowledge was made possible by Lady Dufferin's personal friendship with the then Director of Kew, Sir

Peter Crane.

Of all the ideas gleaned from such eminent horti-culturalists, perhaps the most beneficial has been the adoption of mulching circles around trees and shrubs. These have a threefold benefit: they obviate the need to mow or strim close to trunks, which in turn means less compaction of the soil, less competition from grass and weeds and the decomposing mulch feeds the subject plant and encourages worm activity.

Now that she is away, Lady Dufferin has left a huge void in Clandeboye. She was forever buzzing around, keeping everybody motivated, putting forward her ideas and views and at the same time often ready for a philo-sophical discussion, sometimes even a political one! She would frequently request me to "call by the library door for a beer and a chat" which could last for fifteen or twenty minutes but many times far longer.

While I was aware that these discussions whittled away at my leisure time, I greatly valued them and the profound trust that Lady Dufferin had for me. They, like herself, are sadly missed!

I also miss the annual compilation of a "wish list" for the gardens. This was very much a joint effort whereby either one of us would find or observe or hear about a plant that would be appropriate for Clandeboye, either through association with the 1st Marquess or geograph-ical location (India, Canada etc) and place it on the list to be purchased the following planting season.

LD would often come with plants seen in Kew or France, indeed anywhere in the temperate world. Then we'd have to research them to see if our conditions at

Clandeboye would be likely to sustain the plant in a healthy condition. If deemed unlikely on any grounds, they'd be eliminated from the list. But many passed this scrutiny and now grow happily, I hope, at Clandeboye.

One of my favourites is Tetracentron sinense, whilst one of Lindy's gems is another oak, Quercus dentata, which has one of the largest and most handsome leaves of all temperate oaks.

It is my hope that, in the years ahead, Clandeboye will continue to flourish in much the way Lady Dufferin envisioned as a working estate, a centre of learning and scientific excellence, a place where young and old alike can be close to nature and where they can get up close and personal to wildlife, plants, fungi, insects and the whole natural biodiversity.

For my own part, it is a total privilege to live and work here in Clandeboye and to be one of the stewards that keep the estate ticking along and hopefully hand it on to the next generation in a good, healthy and sustainable condition.

Two things I shall be eternally grateful to Lady Dufferin for. First, when I was in need of accommodation back in 2007, she didn't hesitate to offer me Helen's Tower. "You can be guardian of the tower." During my nine months in the tower, she renovated a little cottage in the woods which Markéta and I now call 'the Ink Bottle' and have lived there happily ever since.

Secondly, during the ongoing Covid pandemic, she insisted on paying for me to have private treatment to repair a hernia I developed in March 2020.

Had it not been for her intervention, I'd be languishing

on a long NHS waiting list, unable to work and to all intents and purposes on the scrapheap.

So huge, sincere thanks, Lady Dufferin. May you rest in peace.

An Eye for Landscapes

Catherine FitzGerald

Catherine FitzGerald is a landscape designer and gardener. The daughter of the late Knight of Glin, she has designed gardens at Hillsborough Castle and Glenarm Castle. She and her family live at Glin Castle, County Limerick. She has known Lindy all her life.

Clandeboye's landscape, woods, lakes and flowers were Lindy's muses and she painted them every day – often out of the window of her studio or in a shepherd's hut which moved around.

She was a passionate conservationist. Out of the studio window, she looked on to an astonishment of interwoven colour – the broad, species-rich wildflower meadow. She began to create it – with painstaking research – thirty-five years ago.

The view to the lake was a constant inspiration, and recurs in her work again and again. She kept it beautiful and healthy, dredging the shores when it began to get clogged with too many rushes, opening up views through to further stretches of water beyond the island of trees, home to a family of swans. She planted more trees, encouraged wildlife and built bridges to connect the landscape together.

Her painter's eye led everything she did in the garden. When she arrived at Clandeboye in the early sixties, there was already a backbone of garden plantings – rhododendrons and shrubs in Brenda's Garden. But she and Sheridan started at once to build on those beginnings, embellishing them with more unusual and varied specimen trees and shrubs. It was a passion they shared and something they enjoyed doing together.

Later on, Fergus Thompson, her wonderfully kind, calm and knowledgeable head gardener, took over the role and they continued to augment the collection with ever new and fascinating introductions and effective plant combinations.

She seemed to know instinctively what would do well where, and how to use plants to create dramatic visual effects. A splash of red high up here? How about the Chilean fire bush for colour in May? Something interesting for mid-summer? How about the late scented magnolia with the purple stamens? A wilsonii? Or some drama for August – a Eucryphia from Seaforde?

There were always knowledgeable gardener friends at Clandeboye – maybe Thomas Pakenham of tree fame, occasionally with the Director of Kew or Glasnevin thrown in. Many weekends were spent planning different areas with us, her guests, the committee of designers.

At the end of it all, you knew perfectly well she had it all worked out beforehand and knew exactly what she was going to do. No one had come up with a better idea than herself!

First Days at Clandeboye

Gerry Summers

Gerry Summers is the former head gardener at Clandeboye. He knew Lindy for over fifty years.

When Lady Dufferin came to Clandeboye, she got out all the gardening books. We'd sit in the garden room, with all the catalogues, and send an order every year to Hillier's of Winchester.

She was very knowledgeable about the estate and about plants, particularly shrubs. She divided the estate map into 41 sections, and listed all the plants by name. She then placed them all on the map.

What plants she brought back from her travels! Once she went up the Amazon and came back via Florida with a lot of miniature orchids, hidden in her luggage.

She was very friendly, not snobbish. We got on very well. On a wet day up in the garden room, the butler would bring us up a cup of tea.

Lord Dufferin, I remember, didn't like daffodils – he was seen many a day, with a wee hook on the end of the walking stick, knocking the heads off. Other flowers were used for decorating the dining room.

She did her own thing after getting my approval. I remember a big blue cedar, growing outside the kitchen window. She said, "It doesn't go with the deciduous oaks." I came back from holiday to see it cut down.

Clandeboye is in my blood. When Lady Dufferin was ill, she sent me messages, saying she was up for a fight. She didn't make it – it was a very great disappointment. It's not the same since she disappeared.

MY SKINNY-DIPPING AUNT

Chloe Guinness

Chloe Guinness – now Lady Reginald Vane-Tempest-Stewart – is Lindy's niece by her brother Billy Guinness and sister-in-law, Lynn Guinness.

The prospect of a weekend at Clandeboye with Aunt Lindy never failed to fill me with excitement and trepidation. Mainly due to what we were going to be made to do! She would be sure to organise every minute of our stay – not one second was to be wasted in idleness.

However, one particular visit was low key, and it will remain my favourite weekend with her. Just my husband Reg and my children Robin, Amy and Violet. She took us to Helen's Tower. It was a very beautiful summer's day. We discussed all things and we all felt the power of her attention on us, which was such a wonderful combination of childlike curiosity and enthusiasm. She was fascinated even by our domestic life!

It was on our way back that, with evident glee and naughty humour, she decided to take a detour to show us her secret swimming lake. She stripped off entirely to her birthday suit and with merry vigour (aged 73) into the freezing water she went, with whoops of joy at the prospect of frightening the local fisherman – who tactfully rowed away for fear of surprising her ladyship enjoying a swim.

"Come on, Reggie, woo-hoo! Don't be shy, woo-hoo," she cried. I think he did manage to keep his drawers on, just!

One Christmas, my mother-in-law, Doreen Wells, the ballerina, was staying too. We were all ordered to bring tap shoes to have lessons from her. Somehow Lindy did manage to get us all tap-dancing after dinner – seriously, who else could achieve this?

Or the time she handpicked some of her favourite young men and asked only me for the weekend, sweetly attempting to matchmake – no female rivals anywhere near! This amused her greatly. And me of course!

I always left Clandeboye slightly exhausted but enriched. She created such a hive of activity and yet, within that, she made a beautiful space for herself to work at her painting. Her delight in all things was an honour to witness and to be a part of. I wish I could be more like she was. I will miss her always. A great spirit.

THE BIOGRAPHER'S FRIEND

Andrew Gailey

Dr Andrew Gailey is author of the biography of the 1st Marquess of Dufferin and Ava: The Lost Imperialist: Lord Dufferin, Memory and Mythmaking in an Age of Celebrity. *Formerly the Vice-Provost of Eton College, he taught at the school for forty years.*

It seems so odd to write after Lindy's death, for I couldn't think of anyone more alive than she. Others will remember the carefree imagination (is it ever?), the laughter and parties at Clandeboye in the sixties, the enthusiastic artist, gardening with JCBs, the ability to think big and the drive to get things done.

Then there were the many schemes and people she supported – myself included. That the Dufferin biography took so long to write was partly that I didn't want it to end.

Being with Lindy was great fun and often surprising; and it was refreshing too in this cynical age to be with someone with a vision.

Yet it was her courage that struck me most – battling most obviously against the insecurities bred in her upbringing. She had a brain as good as most and liked to surround herself with bright people – experts in their field – but she never quite believed in her being their equal.

She often said that she regretted not going to university; that she was trained for a social world that was disintegrating and lacked the formal education that would give her credibility in the next. One might argue that this was what made her distinctive and open-minded.

Nevertheless it would take courage to stand out against the experts and their proposals; and behind the stern, challenging questions and the overly strong stands she sometimes took lay considerable self-doubt.

And of course, being in the position she was, she continually faced the relentless demands for her time and wealth – pressures she had to bear on her own for forty years. More often than not, she relied on her instincts – and in her agents Dick Blakiston-Houston and John Witchell, and Ian Huddleston she chose well.

But she has left a hole in so many people's lives and no one to express it to.

An Irish Castle Weekend

Nicky Dunne

Nicky Dunne has been the Chairman of Heywood Hill Bookshop in London since 2011.

Chronologically, Lindy was the most senior person staying and by some distance.

It was a weekend party at Ireland's most romantic castle. But the energy she emitted was of a wattage that simply awed and outshone every much younger person there. She was tapping into some unquenchable elemental force that very few discover.

Her art had that quality. You can imagine her in a field amid her cows or lying back under a cloudscape, brush in hand and every bit of her vibrating with energy. Like a great oak she had a root system that connected deeply with the places and people she loved. Beyond those visible roots were finer filaments, alive to many stimulations.

Any encounter with Lindy was memorable. I only knew her as an older lady, when her hearing was on the wane. This meant that she would often invade one's "personal space". This physical intimacy, her very presence, could be a little unnerving but it had the effect somehow of cutting through the normal social conventions. Feeling her gaze, or breath even, was like suddenly landing on a spot-lit stage with a highly attentive audience of one.

Many people imagine themselves great hosts or hostesses. The thought wouldn't have crossed Lindy's mind. (Well, perhaps every now and then.) Unlike them, she actually was a great hostess. Her salon brought together every kind of interesting person.

But also of course she was very often alone. I remember seeing her once on the staircase half-landing of her huge London home in the twilight with the shutters closed, a solitary figure. Somehow she made a virtue out of sustained solitude. She did it by decorating the many separate chambers of her mind in vivid colours, brushstroke by brushstroke. What a lesson to us all.

She also loved people and they loved her back. That Irish weekend, about twenty of us climbed a hill, locally referred to as the mountain. At the top, we huddled for a photograph, taken by our lithe, youngish host. As he bent and contorted himself in tightish trousers to frame the shot, Lindy, eyes ablaze, raised her hands in a tigerish way and let out a memorable primeval roar – "Rrrraaaaaaa" – that ended with her shouting into the wind, "You look so sssssSEXY."

Unforgettable Lindy. There was no one quite like her.

My Dear Neighbour

Randal Antrim

The Earl of Antrim lives at Glenarm Castle, County Antrim, with his family. An asset manager, he is Chairman of Sarasin & Partners.

For over three decades, Lindy was a central figure in the lives of me and my family, both in London and Northern Ireland.

She was a true and constant friend, who was invariably the prime mover and took the initiative to organise parties, lunches, dinners or weekend gatherings at Clandeboye or even Glenarm.

In the formative days of my City career in the early 1990s, when I was attempting to establish my professional credentials, Lindy would regularly ring me up in the office in order to make social arrangements.

Invariably, she called when I was on the phone to a client and so spoke to a colleague asking if she could speak to "Randy" (or sometimes even "Randypops"!), thereby decimating my already rather slim credibility.

I'd eventually call her back when there was a lull in the working day and she would proceed to boom down the phone about whether she could bring a party of assorted grandees and/or aesthetes for lunch three months hence.

Being already quite deaf, Lindy expected one to reply clearly and loudly, which was fairly excruciating when all the minutiae of my social plans with the Marchioness could be overheard.

For the uninitiated, a weekend at Clandeboye was quite a demanding experience. Without Sheridan there to moderate her tendencies, in widowhood Lindy would expect guests to keep pace with her incredibly hectic schedule, which began from the moment breakfast was over.

Estate tours to see her latest ventures and improvements went at breakneck pace and usually included visits to Brenda's Garden, the golf course, the anaerobic digester plant and her prize-winning herd of Holstein dairy cows, followed by lunch at Helen's Tower or the conservatory.

She would shriek "Come on everybody!" at the top of her voice and then the unrelenting regime of activities would commence, irrespective of the weather. Lounge lizards were quickly disabused of any ideas they might have about sidling off to retreat to a comfortable armchair by the fire. It didn't matter whether you were a tycoon or a bolshie teenager – you were expected to keep up.

Her character seemed to oscillate between being either incredibly grand or incredibly earthy. The down-to-earth painter and conservationist who greatly enjoyed long spells of relative solitude at Clandeboye could metamorphose in an instant into a grand society hostess from another era. Her parties at Holland Villas Road were legendary and always enormous fun.

This contradiction in her character would sometimes manifest itself in Lindy-esque statements such as:

"Randypops – I'm so rich, you know. If I decided to try and spend it all, starting tomorrow, I don't think I could get through it all!" Followed one month later by: "Randypops – I'm so poor, you know I can barely afford to keep the show on the road at Clandeboye." Only she could somehow get away with making such remarks and not cause one to feel irritated.

Shortly after the Iron Curtain came down, I joined a party of friends, including Lindy, to go on a tour of Czechoslovakia and Hungary, ending up in Vienna. It was a memorable tour, which included many highlights.

Lindy genuinely preferred the more gritty side of the travel experience and was never happier than when we stayed with friends of friends in their tiny flat and camped on the floor of a brutalist apartment building in Prague.

When we eventually got to Vienna, we arranged to have a celebratory lunch in a Michelin-starred restaurant next to the Schwarzenberg Palace. I was in my early twenties and, as lunch was getting near to the end, I remember feeling increasingly anxious about how big the bill was going to be.

While the *chariot des desserts* was being wheeled away, as if by magic Lindy announced rather loudly, "This is the sort of ghastly place Daddy forced me to go to as a child. So I'm afraid I'm going to make you all feel *really* miserable by insisting on paying for the bill myself!"

Our feeble protestations were brushed aside and Lindy's indomitable will prevailed.

Lindy was a force of nature, whose character was

partly honed by the extraordinary collision of formative experiences in her early life.

I will continue to miss her infectious enthusiasm and her generosity of spirit. Along with all those lucky enough to know her, I will remember her for lifting us all up and bringing so much fun and joy into our lives.

A Whirl of Activity

Karen Kane

Karen Kane is in charge of events at Clandeboye, where she has worked for twenty years.

I still expect her to bounce into my office with her wellies on, her coat collar still not unfolded and her cap at a tilt!! It's just so very hard to believe that she has left us.

My very first introduction to Lady Dufferin was back in the early 1990s when I was involved with Conservation Volunteers. It was then in 2003 when I joined the payroll of Clandeboye Estate, helping out with events, a role which grew into me being responsible for all events at the Courtyard.

Lady Dufferin was always very interested in what was going on and, when she had house guests at the weekend, she would bring them round to the Courtyard to meet me and see the Banqueting Hall set up. Through this, I met some wonderful and interesting people.

On another occasion, her house guests were all invited to visit Glenarm Estate in County Antrim.

With a plan to have everyone travel together, I borrowed a Conservation Volunteers minibus and drove the guests to their destination, with Lady Dufferin shouting directions in one ear and her good friend Sean

Rafferty, presenter of Radio 3's *In Tune*, shouting alternative directions in my other! Thankfully we got there eventually.

I have lots of great memories of times spent in the company of Lady Dufferin. We had afternoon teas with Van Morrison and James Galway. On another occasion, I was introduced to her good friend Jools Holland and she organised, very kindly, for me to have two tickets for his Belfast concert. We also went together to the Seamus Heaney Centre to see a Van Morrison concert and I remember Lady D getting her phone out to take photographs, when photography was NOT permitted!

Every August, when we had the Camerata classical music festival, at the end of each concert we would meet at the bar for a chat and put the world to rights. Lady D would have a lager or two and then head over home for a very late supper.

We were also invited along to an event held in Bangor as part of the Aspects Festival. It was to be held in a yurt and drinks were being served on arrival. On the way. Lady D asked me will there be any beers? Thinking it would just be some form of bubbly on offer, she asked if we could stop at an off-sales to get some! This I refused to do as I said we were not going to arrive with a 'carry out'!

On arrival, true enough – it was bubbly but, being "in-the-know", they promptly sent someone off to acquire some beers for the lady. I might add, she was the life and soul of the party. Another event, held in the Banqueting Hall as part of the Aspects Festival, was the

Mad Hatter's Tea Party which Lady D embraced with open arms and dressed accordingly. Mad Hatter she was indeed!

Over the years, we have had various programmes going on at Clandeboye and Lady D became very much involved. For example, students and senior members of staff from Kew Gardens came to stay for a week and we organised various activities such as garden tours etc and Lady D was very much at the forefront. We had the Reading Party programme where students from Queen's University Belfast and Trinity College Dublin came together for a literary week. Lady D was very much the instigator of this event. It was very sociable, with Lady D entertaining the group in her own home.

I remember one occasion when we decided we should have a lunch party for the Clandeboye agent John Witchell's 65th birthday. Lady D thought that would be a great idea and decided we should have it in my house! I had recently moved into my new home and she thought it would be a great opportunity to visit – so she got her phone out to make a guest list. Only to be reminded that my dining table only seats eight! All went well and we had a lovely time.

Over the last year of her life, due to the pandemic, Lady Dufferin spent most of her time at Clandeboye, which meant there was seldom a day when she wasn't out and about around the estate and we spent more time together. We would think up various schemes like new kitchens, redecorating etc. We weren't safe to be let off the lead!

I have very fond memories of Lady Dufferin. My time spent with her during the months before her death and whilst she was in hospital is very memorable, as we talked about her childhood and mine and how very different they had been. Her frail stature reminded me of my late mother and grandmother and her strong determination and fighting spirit was similar to theirs.

Back in 2009, she gave me a painting for my birthday that she had done of my youngest son. I shall treasure it for ever.

I had much correspondence from her hospital bed and I was very distraught when the plans for her homecoming never came to fruition, though in my heart I knew she would have found it hard to be confined to the house. We miss her presence very much at Clandeboye.

Our English Mother

Ana Gama

Ana Gama was Lindy's housekeeper at Holland Villas Road for the last seven years of her life. Lindy adored her, her partner, Miguel Nunes, and their little daughter, Carolina, born in 2018 and brought up at Holland Villas Road.

Lindy wrote in her diary, "I feel so fortunate in that Carolina and Ana and Miguel are not unlike an extended family – they are wonderful to live with."

I thought I would write something about the most wonderful moments with the most kind, loving, intelligent, and caring person I had the privilege to meet and look after, Lady Dufferin.

It has been over a year since she left us all, with our hearts broken, feeling so empty and really sad. I still feel numb about everything and find it really hard to come to terms with our loss.

She was wonderful to so many people here in London, at Clandeboye and around the world. She was a very inspirational person with so much to give and do, so many projects and so many ideas to be accomplished.

What now? What happens next? We must just grieve. There is emptiness, sadness and a big question mark as to why was she taken from us so soon.

But God doesn't do things by half. He needed her.

That's why he called for her. In a sad way, it was good – so she wouldn't suffer with this horrible illness. She wouldn't have been a very good patient, as we all well know.

This larger-than-life woman was for me like a mother. My partner, Miguel, and I used to call her our English mother.

And she really was. She embraced us and took us under her wing and said so many times, "We can do this." We loved and respected her so much. We just hope we have never let her down!

I remember a couple of the many memorable moments with our English mother, Lady Dufferin.

One day, driving Lady D from the dentist, we were at the traffic lights, waiting for them to change. This person started to knock on the car window. Lady D asked me what he wanted. I replied, "He is homeless."

Lady D told me she'd been mistaken for being homeless that day. As we all know, she wasn't one to be tidy all the time, being a painter!

She had gone that morning to the paint shop in very old shorts, with frail, knee-high socks and open-toed sandals. She was not looking at all good.

Then she said this very grand lady approached her and handed out a £20 note, thinking Lady D was homeless.

Lady D said to her, in her sweet and well-spoken voice, "I think I don't want to accept, thank you." When she told me this, we both laughed so much in the car. Little did the lady know that our Lady D was very grand also!

Another time, in spring 2017, we were in the garden working. Lady D told us to carry on while she popped out. She was gone for a good hour or so.

Then Miguel – "head gardener", as she used to call him – said to me, "Would you like a ride in the wheelbarrow around the pond?"

Of course I said yes. After going around four or five times, I was laughing so hard. All of a sudden, I saw Lady D at the stairs window. I was laughing so hard the words didn't come out to say she was at the window watching us. After a bit, I managed to say "She is at the window!"

She didn't mention anything when she came to us in the garden. And we carried on working.

When I fell pregnant with our beautiful daughter Carolina, I asked Lady D if I could speak with her.

When I began to say I was pregnant, she said straightaway, "When I saw you on the wheelbarrow, I knew this was going to happen!"

But of course she was so happy for us. And I can say she loved her "granddaughter Carolina", too.

So many sweet loving memories and moments. Seven years with pure joy and laughter. I learnt so much from this amazing person. I make no apology for bragging about how wonderful she was.

I hope her legacy lives on and on. May she rest in peace in the place she loved the most, next to her beloved husband and near her Clandeboye family.

I miss Lady Dufferin dearly. With so much sadness.

I will come and spend some time with you soon. Until we meet again, my beautiful soul.

THE GREAT POLLINATOR

Francis Russell

Francis Russell was Head of the International Old Master Picture Department at Christie's.

No one who had the fortune to know Lindy Dufferin will forget her. She was effervescent, generous and perceptive, if at times maddening: she had magic.

I was no more than an acquaintance of Sheridan, but his courtesy made an immediate impression, as did his scholarly interest in sporting pictures.

Lindy I met only after she was widowed. She was, as the Italians say, like parsley, seen everywhere and widely loved. The fixed gaze of her questing eyes left one in no doubt of her attention and at times her questions seemed almost too insistent.

The first time Lindy invited me to stay at Clandeboye, at three months' notice, her plans changed at the last minute, as she told me at Nin Ryan's ninetieth birthday party: I had already bought the air ticket and was slightly put out!

But it was at Clandeboye that one sensed something of the kaleidoscope of Lindy's life. The library was the emotional centre of the house, although there was rarely time to look at the early books.

In any case, I was more fascinated by the smaller room with the Viceroy's personal library near the entrance at what was effectively the back of the house. Here one was transported to the world of the 1st Marquess, writer of *Letters from High Latitudes* (1857), with its pioneering account of the Arctic, Norwegian, volcanic island of Jan Mayen, one of the peaks of which was first climbed by my father. Dufferin's acute observations of Iceland, Jan Mayen and Spitzbergen won instant success and became a bestseller.

The large dining room and the drawing room, where tea appeared, were on the east side of the house, overlooking the garden with its majestic clumps of gunnera and the trees framing the lake beyond.

A favourite game was "playing houses". On one occasion, when he and I had been over for the Arts Panel of the National Trust, the collector Christopher Gibbs was commandeered to rearrange the furniture in the drawing room, a task for which he was uniquely qualified. Tables and chairs and carpets were shifted and then rearranged until he and Lindy were satisfied; and the rest of us considered that we deserved our tea.

There was much laughter; and I couldn't but remember an excursion to Castletown, County Kildare, with Lindy's Guinness cousins from Knockmaroon. Mariga Guinness was waiting, put out by changes her husband Desmond, the great saviour of Ireland's buildings, had instituted in her absence. A dozen of us went through the house lugging substantial bits of furniture from room to room, never once retracing our steps. Under Chrissy's practised eyes, the game at Clandeboye was more controlled.

Lindy was never short of things to show her guests:

her cattle; a new golf course; or an exhibition space in an outbuilding.

On my first visit, we lunched at Helen's Tower, which entailed a proper walk through the policies. I set out with an old friend, the actor, the late Julian Sands, Lindy's nephew by marriage. He told me that he was about to go to the Caucasus to climb with a friend whose grandfather had been on Everest in 1922.

I told him that mine had reached a record height on the expedition: he asked his name and when I replied "George Finch", told me that he was his friend's grandparent. Lindy loved putting people together and that my "cousin" Charles Finch became a friend is due to her.

Lindy enjoyed laying on expeditions for her guests. She might take us to Killyleagh – so umbilically linked to Helen's Tower and with equally memorable views – or Mount Stewart.

Once we went to the Montgomerys at Grey Abbey, to find a party as varied as Lindy's own: the charming son of one of the Rolling Stones and that champion of the Anglo-Irish house, Mark Bence-Jones, who with his daughter and very little help from me demolished a large sponge cake.

Lindy laid out her plans with due care. On one occasion, she decided to arrange a weekend for her kinsman John Guinness, iconographer extraordinary.

I was unable to think of any house with serious portraits within easy reach that he wouldn't know. So Lindy asked where I would most like to go: Seaforde, I replied, having heard how wonderful the demesne is.

Lindy rang Lady Anthea Forde to ask if she could

bring ten of us, to be told that she couldn't arrange a lunch party, as she herself would only return from London the night before.

Lindy had got the bit between her teeth, would not be put off and said she would arrange everything.

She did. Provisions, crockery, glasses and cutlery were dispatched from Clandeboye with two maids and Lindy's chef who commandeered the kitchen. Seaforde more than lived up to reputation; and John was happy to see copies of the pictures an early Victorian Forde had admired in Florence rather than portraits in need of identification.

Lindy had an instinct for mixing people. At a party during the Edinburgh Festival she told me that I was a "pollinator". Asked what she meant, she replied someone who introduced people to others who would interest them.

Some time later, she asked me to suggest names for a party she planned in Holland Villas Road. Very sensibly, she quickly realised that her great friend Christopher Balfour would be much more helpful than I could be. The party Lindy gave with his help every July was for many a highlight of the year.

Travel was important to Lindy. She loved her visits to Morocco and regularly stayed with the Channons, Paul and Ingrid, on Mustique. One January she returned, surprised that no fewer than four of her young Guinness cousins – all, as she said, beautiful and clever and rich – were as yet unmarried.

Soon after her return, she found herself next to Hylton Murray-Philipson at a dinner party. She saw that he was good-looking and intelligent and established that he was rich and unmarried. She then asked if he would recruit three friends in the same position for a dinner with her cousins in Holland Villas Road, inviting Anna Gendel, Chrissy and myself, as it were, as spectators. Much laughter was had, but no matches were made.

Emotionally generous as Lindy was, she could be scratchy, even aggressive, particularly on the rare occasions when she came to a "picnic" in my flat. Once, as we arrived at a fiftieth birthday party in Dorset, she was surprisingly fractious.

Lindy had two enduring preoccupations: her painting; and the future of Clandeboye. Painting was much more than a pastime; it was Lindy's refuge from her many responsibilities. She surely knew at heart that she was not a great artist like, say, her friend David Hockney, to whom she sat on numerous occasions.

Her style changed. Her early work, as she knew, gravitated to the bedrooms of the houses of friends and relations. I personally admired most the landscapes that reflected her study of early nineteenth-century *plein air* oil sketches and still regret not buying one of her views of the early tombs at Pantalica, painted when she was staying with Giuseppe di San Giuliano in Sicily.

Lindy loved painting in the Burren and still more at Clandeboye where her cattle inspired a series of pictures. Painting was in a sense an escape.

By contrast, Lindy knew that the future of Clandeboye must be an enduring commitment. She rehearsed ideas with many. She did not have an exaggerated opinion of the architectural merits of the house, but she was fully aware of its exceptional historic interest.

Many friends were asked to write brief paragraphs to express our sense of the significance of the place, but none of us was in any doubt that Lindy herself understood this more clearly than anybody else.

Lockdown meant that Lindy spent six months at Clandeboye in 2020. For so committed a traveller this was an unprecedented span, as she wrote in an email in response to one from me telling her of John Guinness's death: "It is extraordinary to be in one place for so long." Painting was giving her "great pleasure" and she planned a "show": yet she wanted to know what I was "thinking about" and doing "and about Christie's and all that". Less than a fortnight later, she was in hospital with incurable cancer.

Lindy was an inspired interrogator. Her unyielding gaze made it all but impossible not to answer her at times very direct questions. But she was genuinely interested in the responses; and this was not the least of the measures of her friendship.

How she quickened the pace of so many lives.

The Dancing Queen of Istanbul

Ömer Koç

Ömer Koç is a Turkish businessman, art collector and chairman of Koç Holding and chairman of the board of trustees of Koç University. He is a sponsor of the Istanbul Biennial, the contemporary art exhibition.

I just wanted to share with you a photograph taken of Lindy at the Biennial party (see plate sections) I gave in Istanbul in 2019. I think it captures her spirit brilliantly!

I remember her dancing away the night, mostly barefoot, at the private residence of the last Caliph of the Ottomans. She really was the life and soul of that 600-person party.

Even people who did not know her came up to me and asked who that elderly, discalced woman, dancing with such enthusiasm and abandon was.

It is all the more remarkable when one bears in mind that she used to say that every sonar impression, she heard in a metallic way!

I think that Biennial party was her last big outing. She always brought so much life and energy to anything she attended! I am so happy she took the trouble to attend our three-night opening. Who could have known at the time that it was a farewell of sorts?

Lindy was one of those rare creatures who lived life voraciously, to the full. Always goaded by curiosity, intellectual and otherwise, she had such appetite and zest for what life had to offer!

Her irreverent and at times deadpan sense of humour was so refreshing, especially in today's ghastly cancel culture and oppressive political correctness.

I am sure she is being missed enormously by those who came into contact with her. Requiescat in pace! She will continue to live in her friends' hearts and imagination.

THE 1ST MARQUESS'S GRANDFATHER CLOCK

Graham Little

Graham Little is a writer, broadcaster and producer. He lives in Northern Ireland with his family and their grandfather clock. His children attend the Nature Rangers Forest School at Clandeboye.

What does one wear to a small private film premiere in a stately home?

I considered that question against the experience of my first visit to the same stately home, when I was summoned to the library for afternoon tea and the host had surprised me by crashing in through the French doors wearing muddy hiking boots, purple tracksuit bottoms and a checked shirt with a tweed jacket.

Just like her dual names, that outfit perfectly encapsulated the character and life of Lindy Guinness, or Lady Dufferin. She'd been out planting trees on her beloved Clandeboye Estate that morning, and would be painting scenes from it that evening. So, the bottom half was her as hands-on land steward, and the top half was her as bohemian artist.

A few weeks before that first meeting, I had sent a speculative letter outlining our plans to make a documentary on the voyages of the 1st Marquess of Dufferin and Ava, the remarkable Frederick

Hamilton-Temple-Blackwood, previous owner of Clandeboye and an ancestor of Lindy's late husband. I requested an interview with her and permission to film in the house.

She politely invited me up to discuss it, but then equally politely said she didn't like being interviewed and was too busy enjoying her "wonderful life" to open it to the intrusion of television creators and audiences. But although we were thus denied the sparkling contributor and astonishing museum location I had hoped for, she did pledge the support of her archivist, Lola Armstrong, to help us with research, and I kept Lindy appraised by sending postcards from various obscure locations like the Outer Hebrides, and Svalbard.

When the film was finished, she wanted the first viewing to be at Clandeboye, and arranged a gathering one Sunday afternoon. Although our relationship at this point had mostly been conducted by postcards and email, I was already hugely fond of her and winning her approval of the film was more important to me than winning the approval of the BBC, who were paying for it. So, I dressed up for the occasion and arrived at Clandeboye at the appointed hour with a DVD and a few bottles of wine.

And of course, like on previous and subsequent visits, I was immediately swept along by the strong current that was Lindy's irresistible energy and zest, which picked up everything in its path and brought all and sundry to wherever she was headed. In this instance, where she was headed was down to the cellars. There was an eclectic group of us shuffling along in her wake, including a surveyor from Christie's and a university historian. And me, in my nice suit, now descending into centuries of dusty history to help her move and catalogue priceless furniture and treasures.

In one alcove, a single bulb cast a low light the colour of old newspapers and faintly illuminated an extraordinary array of items including an ancient Abyssinian stone tablet; huge portraits including one of her notorious mother-in-law, Maureen Guinness; antique golf clubs; and a lonely-looking Grandfather clock leaning precariously against a wall, draped in cobwebs.

"Oh that's lovely," I said.

"Do you like it?" I *thought* she said.

"Yes," I replied.

"Stick a note on that clock with Graham's name on it," demanded Lady D of the Christie's agent, who trailed behind her with a pen and some post-its.

It turned out she had actually asked me, "*Would* you like it?" rather than "*Do* you like it."

I was dumbfounded.

"Irish-made, around 1840s," whispered the Christie's agent in my ear, nodding conspiratorially. 1840s, and therefore almost certainly once the property of my great hero, the 1st Marquess, who inherited Clandeboye in 1841.

I stammered an uncertain thank you, assuming I had misunderstood. But as we emerged blinking into the daylight an hour or so of furniture removing and cataloguing later, Lindy implored me to arrange the collection of "my" clock immediately, before turning her attentions to tea, and then the film viewing.

The tea was as entertaining and surprising as I came to expect on each visit, with Lady D expertly directing conversation and apportioning airtime like the conductor of an orchestra. The screening was less successful. There were various technological challenges with the DVD player and the TV, the wine enhanced the post-prandial slump, and the film is long and probably boring. Lady D fell asleep at one point.

As I sat in that beautiful old room, each of us guests pretending to be interested in the film and pretending not to notice Lindy's nodding head, I considered the contrast between her and the 1st Marquess. He lived for pomp and ceremony, and was so acutely conscious of status, of history, of legacy, that he built a museum to himself and his adventures in Clandeboye.

But, with Lindy, the past was barely ever mentioned, never mind celebrated. Her focus seemed always on the present and on the future. She didn't do pomp and ceremony, and a clock from the 1840s should not stand idle in a museum if it could go and work in someone's living room.

We got it restored, but as a means of keeping time it of course struggles to match our various digital devices for accuracy. But keeping time is, to me, the least important of its functions. Keeping a connection to my two favourite Dufferins is the primary and priceless role of that old clock.

A Mother and Daughter Write

Georgie and Honor Fanshawe

Georgie and Honor Fanshawe are the daughter and granddaughter of Paul Channon (1935–2007), later Lord Kelvedon, the MP and Cabinet Minister who was a cousin and great friend of Lindy and Sheridan. He gave the address at Sheridan's memorial service.

Georgie Fanshawe

Lindy was a friend of my parents and a great part of my childhood. She was married to my father's cousin, Sheridan.

After my parents died, Lindy became a particular friend of mine and would often come and stay with us. Whenever she did, she would bring extraordinary presents – Moroccan slippers with curly toes, a strange, unwearable Egyptian tunic, a beautiful picture of a bird, and one of a fish, by Simon Bussy.

Lindy seemed to know about everything. She once took my son Oli (aged ten) and our cousin Tania Kindersley around Westonbirt Arboretum. They came back looking traumatised. The walk had gone on for hours at a very fast pace and she had made them learn the Latin name of every tree they passed and had tested them again in the car on the way home.

One wet weekend I got my car stuck in mud on the lawn, and for ages I tried to reverse it out, but the car wouldn't move and the wheels kept spinning. Lindy walked by and offered to help. She got in the car and moved it forward a bit and immediately managed to drive it off the wet lawn. She looked triumphant and I felt grateful and a bit cross.

She came and stayed with us in Mustique for Christmas a couple of times. Every morning, she would get up at around six and make a pot of tea and take it back to her bed, while she wrote her diary. Then she would set off with her rucksack and explore the island and draw and paint.

She would come back at nine and would normally say, "Well! I have had the most remarkable morning."

Wherever we went on Mustique, Lindy would always want to bicycle. Most times she would take my daughter Ella's bike. Sometimes Ella wanted to bike herself. So eventually I rented Lindy another bike, but it wasn't as smart as Ella's and Lindy didn't look very enthusiastic about it.

The next day, when we were going to the beach, Ella came out and her bike was missing again and the old, battered one that I had rented was sitting outside the house.

As we all know, for a large part of her life, Lindy was very deaf, but she still managed to join in most conversations. But sometimes, she would look a bit sad and you could see in her eyes that she really longed to properly hear what was going on.

One evening at home, I remember my brother saying about someone we all knew, "I really loathe that bloody idiot!"

Lindy turned to me and said, "What did he say?"

"He said he doesn't like him very much," I told her.

And my brother shouted, "No, I bloody didn't. I said I bloody loathe him," and Lindy roared with laughter.

Lindy loved to dance and I remember one New Year in Mustique, she and I, Anne Glenconner and Dora Loewenstein danced under the moonlight, in the shallows of the sea, for hours and hours.

I am so glad I have letters and photos and the pictures she gave me to remind me of her, and the Egyptian tunic. I knew she was ill, but it was a great shock to hear that she had died. She had an amazing energy and I always felt she was the most alive person I had ever met.

That is how I will remember her.

Honor Fanshawe (born 2008)

I can't really remember much about my godmother Lindy.

I just remember she was clever and sweet, but somehow a little daunting. She always gave me exotic gifts like pillows with camels on them, and I remember I always opened them on Christmas Eve by candlelight, which made them so much more exciting.

But really the first word that comes to mind when

I think of Lindy is art. I remember lying on a daybed drawing some palm trees with her and feeling envious of how she managed to make realistic shapes with just a couple of strokes. When I showed her my art and told her it was the first time I had ever managed to draw a good palm tree, she replied with, "Well, good for you," which made me and her laugh.

I always liked her hair which reminded me of a cloud streaked with copper, with curls bobbing everywhere. When I stayed with her in Ireland, all I remember was a big house with stone floors and weapons on the walls and Lindy greeting each cow we met on our walks like an old friend.

In the first lockdown, we sent each other letters, and I had to write down all my favourite books and tell her about them. I always tried very hard at the little drawings on the envelopes that I did. I wanted her to know that my art had come a long way from the scribbles of a palm tree I did all those years ago.

Lindy shows the way, Clandeboye, 2020.

Having a Go

Ian Huddleston

Sir Ian Huddleston is a Judge of the High Court of Northern Ireland and a Trustee of the Clandeboye Estate. He gave the address at Lindy's funeral at Clandeboye in 2020.

"Come for tea."

From that innocent invitation my friendship and, from it, my admiration for Lindy began.

They were inauspicious beginnings – set around that rickety card table before the roaring fire in the library at Clandeboye. But it is the place I now most associate with Lindy and indeed with the heart of Clandeboye itself. Just like so many others.

We had a very "nice" tea followed by a beautiful walk around the lake and so I was selected to be her lawyer. Not, at that stage, the estate's lawyer but rather the one who was to look after her personal affairs. Her minder. She'd had a few unfortunate experiences and felt she needed one.

As was Lindy's wont, we got straight to the thorny issue of economics. It was beautifully done. A story about how her last lawyer had invited her to a wonderful lunch but had made the cardinal sin of including the time spent on his next bill. A point not missed by the beady marchioness...

And so we hit upon an unorthodox lawyer/client arrangement: most of our consultations would be conducted either over supper at Holland Villas Road (when we were both in London) or over long walks at Clandeboye (when we were both in Ireland).

Save where there was an actual "transaction", money would not pass hands so that we each could be uninhibited in our respective inputs! She was liberated from the fear of hourly rates. I was (theoretically) liberated as to an honesty of view – whether it was actually heeded or not.

The suppers became more and more leisurely, the walks longer and the relationship deeper until there was very little, indeed if anything, that we did not share with one another.

That was easy for Lindy because she has always had the capacity for curiosity, openness and warmth – a feature that endeared her to so many – but more difficult for me as a rather closed Ulsterman. She drew me out, like so many others who have contributed to this collection – in spite of myself and, as I reflect upon it now after her death, much more so than I had even realised at the time.

On my part, the admiration grew from the start. I truly admired the spirit in which she had embraced Clandeboye and its people from her earliest days in 1964 when she first came there, but more particularly following Sheridan's death in 1988, when she came to own it. As I said at her funeral, the place and the people that make up Clandeboye very much became her surrogate family.

There is a saying of the Anglo-Irish, widowed, land-owning class – one coined by the author Elizabeth Bowen but that's oft repeated – which suggests that "Irish widows" of that ilk are happiest on a boat (as it would have been then), heading either from Ireland back to London (and implicitly civilisation) or towards Ireland (with its quieter allure) – but that the dilemma for those same widows was that they were never quite sure in which direction they preferred the boat to be travelling...

Typically, Lindy had no such dilemma. She embraced both aspects of her life with equal fervour. As I was working at the lawyers Farrer & Co at the time, she and I did the BA commute together very often – usually by accident. Me scrupulously following the rules for on-time and easy boarding (with no luggage) – she carrying anything from plant cuttings from Fergus for the London garden (or vice versa) to poorly wrapped chunks of blood-leaching venison or dripping pheasants destined for her London table or the 'better' cheeses going the other way – and all carried in her commodious canvas handbag.

She was rarely stopped or questioned. If she ever was, she immediately deployed "that" charm we all would immediately recognise and, so, sail through. It was remarkable given that, even pre-Brexit and "the Protocol", there were quite strict rules around the importation of plant and/or food products to/from NI. The canvas handbag may not have met the Lady Bracknell test but the aplomb certainly did!

From my perspective, many others in Lindy's position

would have left Clandeboye to its fate following Sheridan's death – sold up and headed to the Beau Rivage or an equivalent off-shore haven. That life she would have absolutely hated but it gave me plenty of ammunition with which to tease her – it would have been, after all, perfect from a tax-planning perspective. Indeed, on one occasion on a trip to see "the gnomes" in Zurich, she said – VERY LOUDLY – as we approached passport control in Switzerland, "Darling, I bet they think that I'm your mother and that we are on our way to Dignitas." What could I do but laugh at the look of utter bemusement on the faces of the border guards?

Instead of taking what would have been any easier option (or indeed the sage tax planning advice), she told me how Sheridan in the last stages of his life encouraged her to "Have a go" with Clandeboye – with the caveat that, if she ever found she wanted another life, she was to sell up immediately and move on. He wrote to her in those very terms on his deathbed – a letter that still exists secreted amongst her most precious possessions.

She never found another option that appealed to her more and in adopting Clandeboye was – to the end – happy with the choice that she made.

I've always admired Lindy for having that go (which in itself involved considerable effort) – but, much more than that, in having so many other "goes" over the last thirty-plus years over a wide range of projects and ideas. She was remarkable for being able to maintain her indomitable spirit and enthusiasm for Clandeboye's future, not just throughout her life but in the plans she made for it into the future and how it should benefit others.

She used the same phrase to me – "Let's have a go" – in September 2020 – exactly two weeks before her diagnosis when I asked if she was really **sure** she wanted to sign a £2 million contract to build the new yoghurt factory at Clandeboye in the face of what was to be a significant birthday.

She used the same phrase again to her amazed doctors when I met with them to discuss whether or not it made sense for her to commence immunotherapy to treat the cancer which by then had invaded her body.

I still have such a vivid recollection of the startled look on the face of the young NHS registrar – who clearly had never met anyone quite like her – as she said to him in what was by then, I must admit, a rather tired and strained voice, "But, darling, we have to have a go!"

However one looks at it, those words encapsulated a spirit that many others half her age might have lost in the midst of life's vicissitudes but which Lindy retained right to the end.

In the particular case of Clandeboye, having a go was not an easy choice. Ulster throughout the sixties and seventies and, even into the more normalised world of the eighties, held many bear traps for the unwary – ranging along the ambit of religion, history (and with it the particular aspects of Irish and colonial history upon which Clandeboye is based) to the more obvious (and immediate) security risks. Traps which sadly still exist.

Lindy was (or rather chose to be) oblivious to those traps – traps which have felled so many others – and opted not only to have a go but to make Clandeboye her home and carve out a life in Northern Ireland – one that very much suited her.

One can easily see why. In the unspoiled beauty of Clandeboye and its history, she found both a peace and a stability that possibly wasn't available to her elsewhere. Within the environment of the estate, her creativity flourished – there are not many of her series of works that do not have a major focus on the house, the estate with its lakes and 19th-century landscape – or even, more pertinently, her beloved cows!

If one needed further evidence of that, look no further than at the 162 canvases which she painted during the lockdown period between March and September 2020.

Her contentment was such that, to my certain knowledge, she left the estate on a maximum of six occasions during that period. I was concerned that she might have been lonely but she constantly assured me – and I did believe her – that she was (to use her words) "blissfully happy" during those days in her (2,000-acre) "playpen", as she would call it.

If she did feel any hint of the black dog approaching (and inevitably it did happen) she would simply "remove her ears", as she referred to her cochlear implants, have a couple (or perhaps more) of her favourite "little beers" and paint into the wee small hours.

During that period, she also read avidly – and extensively. In the long days of her last summer, she "found" process philosophy. To quote Heraclitus on that theme, "Everything changes and nothing remains still." In hindsight, how apt.

When I called, I would find her reading on the terrace on a resurrected wicker lounger from the thirties – which she had found in one of the stables and had mended – her golf visor firmly in place as a protection from the weather, be it sun, rain or wind.

She would have a pencil or highlighter firmly in hand and before the ensuing walk/lunch/afternoon tea/ pre-dinner drink or supper – or sometimes all of them – we would sit while she explained the most recent revelation and how that revelation was improving her painting and giving her added perspective in her work.

She would invariably then share the Instagram posts which evidenced that transformation and (modestly) revel in the number of "likes" the latest work had garnered. In that context, it is not perhaps surprising how she managed to paint the 162 canvases or accrue the crates of empty beer bottles that went hand in hand with that creative process.

Her reading continued to be a solace after her diagnosis. Not for her, however, the classics or something uplifting as one might have thought! No. I was despatched to Clandeboye to find a copy of Montaigne – dissect it into manageable chunks (by size rather than content), rebind it with duct tape and bring it back to her.

On the increasingly rare occasions when I was allowed to visit by that stage (given tightening restrictions) our discussions could range to Montaigne but could as easily follow on from an article in the press that day. The headlines in the *FT* one weekend prompted a largely rhetorical debate as to how one might tackle the reported corruption in the Vatican. "Beyond our paygrade," I suggested, sitting beside her hospital bed whilst we both had one of her yoghurts. Instead we turned to an article in the same paper about some erotic drawings by Duncan Grant which had then just been gifted to Charleston and, so, her thoughts on her own collection.

Given her position at that time, I might have opted for topics that were much lighter or more self-indulgent. But the phrase "Do not go gentle into that good night" was definitely the guiding light by which she operated – not just in relation to her reading choices but in relation to her medical treatment and her determination overall. She remained determined to fight.

In hindsight, September and October 2020 were awful months as those fights played out. But I think we all can derive huge comfort from the fact that, during the early days of that preceding summer, she was truly happy. Part of that happiness undoubtedly derived from purpose. She'd embarked upon projects she'd wanted to do for a very long time.

The stables enjoyed an Augean purge. Bonfires ensued and rats (quite literally) scurried away – more afraid of her ladyship than the gardeners (who in turn were frightened of the rats).

Late planting continued apace. You might have caught the Instagram post of the "Landgirl at Work", with Lindy atop a trailer of manure being driven by Fergus. Anything from the nursery or the garden (or anywhere else) that had not already been rooted was found an appropriate home, inspected and watered on a daily basis.

Almost daily planting parties spread across the estate – all the way from the gardens to Helen's Tower Woods. Those projects occupied her days and painting her nights. She described it to me as her "taking back control" – something which I thought at the time (and still think) as strange, as to me she was the one who always was very much in charge – and posthumously still is!

It was complex – a throwback to her childhood, a rebellion against the "men sitting behind computers, doing God knows what" (an allegation from which I certainly was not exempt) to a finding of liberation in a much more general sense.

I have no doubt she missed her friends and the usual round of socialising London gave her and which she enjoyed so much. But knowing that it wasn't happening in any event possibly soothed away any wistfulness.

More importantly for her – especially as things turned out – she was amongst the people who had known her for most of her adult life and loved and cared for her in their own ways, resonant of that particular balance which often exists within the boundaries of an estate wall, particularly in Ireland. It is a particular type of love, based not on sanguinity but upon love of the place and mutual respect of purpose and endeavour.

Most of her missives to me from her hospital bed were immensely practical but, in one of her more intimate, late-night emails, she shared this with me, entitled *Night Thoughts*:

What I have been learning since I was [sic] in hospital is the idea that the most important thing is to build up one's inner self and learn to rely on this – we believe that happiness is out there in houses and things but actually that is an illusion. [It's] within each of us – everyone has the possibility of finding their most deep and wonderful treasure but we all sit on it and never look inside the box we are sitting on...

Remarkable, given all that was going on with her, and so appropriate for the pandemic world then – and indeed in the chaotic world that has followed it.

Clandeboye and its ways gave Lindy a focus throughout her life but most particularly during lockdown. It allowed the space for her to find a reconciliation with life throughout that summer – without knowing what was ahead.

Upon reflection, it was really the culmination of a deep and thoughtful life packed with experiences of every type – a "fantastically full one", as her brother Billy described it to me – a description that no one who knew or even came in contact with her can deny.

She in turn throughout her time there gave Clandeboye and its people a particular ideology, a focus and a distinct but very personal energy. In short, she imbued it and them with her "can do" spirit and the confidence to "have a go" – a spirit for which she was famous not just locally but around the globe, as the tributes that followed her death confirmed.

It is that spirit that I now feel is acutely missing. The

person who, faced with so many options, chose to be the figurehead of an Irish rural estate is gone and the place is undoubtedly bereft without her and her indomitable spirit.

The time I spent with Lindy during lockdown I now look upon as priceless. As a lawyer, I had tried (and frankly often given up trying) to pin all of her ideas down and record them formally. As a friend, during those last months, I was able to explore the estate more fully – ramble with her all over it – and spend that time discussing and debating with her at some considerable length about what she really wanted after her death.

She had heard somewhere that the Oxford colleges have a 500-year business plan and thought that Clandeboye and the Dufferin Foundation – the charity which she had set up with Sheridan – should have one. As I pointed out to her, more than once, that was something of an ambitious target given that neither, at that point, had a 12-month business plan, much less a more adventurous or strategic one.

Undaunted by such trivial details, she, intuitive as ever, and doubtless at some level mindful of her own mortality, developed in conjunction with Dr Annie Tinley the idea of "Lady PRONI" [PRONI being the acronym for the Public Records Office of NI – the state custodian of the Province's historical records].

In Lindy's case, the idea behind "Lady PRONI" was the embodiment of a notional figurehead for Clandeboye that would exist for 500 years (or more). One that was imbued with the spirit of place, ideology and passion of someone, although she was too modest to say it, who embodied more than a passing resemblance of a certain marchioness. An Orlando for North Down, if you will. Someone who, for those who are left behind to implement her wishes, could evolve and give them direction. Someone to prompt them to ask the question "What would Lindy do?" and, in turn, to give them the confidence to "have a go" in the way that she would. A voice in their ear. A prompt.

The next period – as with any estate where there is a "succession event" (as lawyers so tactfully call them) – by necessity will be a period of consolidation.

There are basically three main pillars – Clandeboye as an agricultural estate; the house and the collection; and the Dufferin Foundation as an overarching charity. These are the three pieces of a jigsaw that Lindy's trustees must now fit together – obviously with the help of her recorded wishes but relying also upon the spiritual guidance of Lady PRONI.

In the case of Clandeboye, she very much wanted it to remain much as it is. Not by any means preserved in aspic but as a place where evolution could happen at a slightly gentler pace than elsewhere. Fundamentally, a place that could be protected but simultaneously used to nurture social enterprise, education (for all ages), research and, importantly, act as an exemplar of a sustainable environment of a type that is increasingly rare in these islands. One that has stood the test of time since laid out in the 1800s. A lung for Northern Ireland, as she liked to refer to it – a place which could allow its people to breathe in the widest sense of the meaning of that word physically, emotionally and intellectually.

Indeed it was to ensure that preservation that she felt that the investment in the anaerobic digester and the yoghurt factory was so important. The anaerobic digester as a way to power the estate, just as in days gone by a waterwheel or windmill might have done but to simultaneously provide essential income for reinvestment. The yoghurt factory, in order to allow the yoghurt business to fulfil its full economic potential, vindicate Clandeboye's prize-winning dairy herd and again provide income to help build and improve the estate and sustain it for the longer term.

Lindy was equally conscious, however, that she did not want the estate to be too insular or become stranded as just another rural estate. She wanted it to reach out.

I know from personal experience and she, by intuition, that Northern Ireland is by default guilty of a certain insularity – an insularity that does not serve it well.

Through the Dufferin Foundation, in addition to helping preserve and develop the estate, she hoped that links could be forged across the island of Ireland (tying in the Guinness heritage, which has been such an important legacy to Ireland, the estate and, indeed, in her own life). That the existing links with Great Britain could be strengthened and then carried on further afield – particularly to those places with more historical Dufferin connections – all within a wider charitable context but ultimately as a way of connecting to the wider world.

She hoped that part of her legacy would facilitate those separate "vectors of energy" (as she called them) and promote initiatives that, in participation with other charitable organisations, could achieve things in that wider world – redolent of the achievements of the first Dufferin and Avas – but adapted in this modern age to have more of a health, educational and environmental focus.

Her hopes for Clandeboye and the Dufferin Foundation were that they, acting in tandem with other key charities and bodies, could achieve the same level of success around her passions for the encouragement of education, the development of academic and historical research and above all the promotion of the value of woodlands and the natural environment in ways that would fulfil the charitable objectives of the Foundation.

I am more prosaic than she was but have learned from Lindy that from little acorns oaks do grow. Lindy's love for the Forest Schools Association, with its ethos of integrated education and outdoor learning, is something that is now well rooted at Clandeboye.

I am a total convert to the idea of taking children out of their normal educational and domestic settings to places like Clandeboye which has its own unique energy and introducing them to the natural environment as a new way of learning old skills. It also in turn helps their teachers recapture some basic lost art of understanding the environment in which we all live and which is so important for our collective future and, simultaneously, reintroduce a bit of magic to the learning process. Lindy loved that idea and the energies behind it and loved spending time with the children.

Fund-raising has started to provide a more permanent base on the estate – in the form of a purpose-built eco–school – a project for which Lindy had sought planning permission before her death.

At a research level, the estate is participating in an academic research programme being run across the British Isles to establish the environmental credentials of combining woodland amenity and carbon capture. It now has the Woodland Trust NI, based at Clandeboye, as an important long-term partner.

In the field of education, it was very much Lindy's hope that the links that she had already established between Trinity College Dublin and Queen's University Belfast (which culminated in the famous reading parties) would be strengthened and become more integrated into the cultural life of Northern Ireland and, thus, Ireland more generally.

In the context of the archives, she wanted to encourage academic and historical research. More particularly, she was keen to establish greater links with the Public Records Office for Northern Ireland – PRONI (the body from which the titular figurehead is derived) – and the house. Greater access could be provided to the archives of the 1st Marquess and the, as yet, largely unearthed treasure trove of material that exists at Clandeboye for those keen to understand and put in context the age of empire and the truly remarkable role a diplomat from Northern Ireland played within it, from Canada to India.

With Lindy and Sheridan's modern British and Irish art collection, she was keen that through public exhibitions – both locally and further afield – the long-standing connections they had both enjoyed with institutions such as the Royal Academy, the Wallace Collection and her link to Duncan Grant and the Charleston Legacy (to name but a few) could be strengthened. That her trustees would "leverage" the collection and bring it and, through it, Clandeboye to a greater audience. There, too, dialogue has begun.

That modern collection is an important strand of a story yet to be told, not just through the pictures she and Sheridan jointly or separately amassed – but what they meant to her and can mean to others in terms of personal development.

In one of her other emails to me over this time, she put it thus:

"I have <u>no</u> [her emphasis] need of some reputation because painting has been the vehicle that I have used to structure my life of looking and learning and enjoying the way of life and the kind of people in the art world. I do not want anything back from painting, painting has given me everything."

That is the only story that she wanted to be told. She wanted people less fortunate than she to be inspired to learn to look at life in different and personal ways.

In taking all of those strands together to form that jigsaw, Lady PRONI will very much continue as the figurehead, at the prow of the ship she had spent almost sixty years helming.

The course is one that fundamentally she and Sheridan had jointly mapped out in the charitable objectives of the Dufferin Foundation in 1988 – shortly before his own death. There is no doubt that her lieutenants – both those that are current and those that will come after – will have to trim our sails, to deal with the winds of change that inevitably will come. That is no more than one has to do in any organisation and, for Clandeboye and the Dufferin Foundation, it will be no different.

But, in plotting that course, we still have Lady PRONI and the Founders' Principles which were crafted before her death as a guide. What we all know, however, without any shadow of a doubt, is that the thing that would annoy her most and betray her legacy is not "having a go".

And that is a wrath I, for one, am not prepared to risk encountering in this world or the next.

FAREWELL, LINDY

Charles Cator

Charles Cator is a furniture historian and Deputy Chairman of Christie's International.

I have been thinking very much about dear, wonderful, magical, entrancing Lindy over the last weeks and it is always that beautiful smile and the laughter that come into my mind immediately.

That incredible sense of the joy of life; of giving everything that you have got to give; the passionate interest in such a myriad of different things and subjects; the boundless energy and extraordinary enthusiasm. Our lives were so blessed by knowing her and experiencing her remarkable capacity for friendship.

All these most special qualities were why talking to her was so captivating – however boring one was, she made you feel you were the only person in the world, listening with such intensity and those beautiful eyes so wide open...

Then, in the midst of all the seriousness, she would suddenly make a brilliantly apposite and irreverent observation, followed by peals of laughter.

And of course her voice, as she asked some intensely direct question, innocent and insightful at the same time. She had such an incredible capacity for absorbing information because she actually concentrated and listened. She genuinely wanted to know and was interested in the lives of others. And that came from her great warmth and generosity of heart.

Reading the obituaries reminded me of her childhood and the tailored luxury of her father's world and that struck me again as I have known few more ascetic people than Lindy.

She made sure that Clandeboye and Holland Villas Road were the epitome of luxury for her immensely lucky friends but I always felt that she herself was just not that interested. That gave her a wonderful way of dealing with "grand life", going along with it and very much part of it but always retaining her free spirit, so she was never in its thrall and could come and go as she chose.

And that was echoed in her outfits, immensely elegant in her inimitable, very measured style or equally at home in her painting kit. She had that unique ability to move effortlessly between all worlds, enriching the lives of so many from all walks of life with her charm and generosity of spirit.

One of the many things that I so loved about Lindy was that she was so very modest and self-aware. She never made a fuss and I know that in her extraordinarily varied life she had seen a lot of mega-egos but she had this remarkable quality of inner serenity that radiated out of her.

When Ian Huddleston described, in his brilliant funeral tribute, going to see the cancer specialist and Lindy saying, "I think we've got to give it a go, don't you?" it was so completely Lindy: uncomplaining, courageous, optimistic and practical, as she always was about her deafness.

I am sure that her immense courage in her last days came from her inner serenity and peace. She had been with Sheridan on his journey during his illness and I'm sure that gave her an inner strength.

How brilliantly she coped with life without him and how inspiring was her vision for Clandeboye. Her enthusiasm and passion were unfailing, seeing the life-enhancing role the house and the estate could play in the lives of the people of Belfast and in the whole of Northern Ireland. And how right she was.

Another of Lindy's genius qualities was trust – she always trusted and because of her innate goodness good people responded to her. So she was a brilliant chooser.

And not only was she a brilliant chooser but she was always there, giving unceasing support, encouragement and affection. The great loyalty and respect she inspired at Clandeboye were always a wonder to witness.

I'm sure that, like all her friends, I always think of Lindy as eternally young – her spirit was so strong. It seems so cruel that someone so vital, so dynamic, so precious to so many who loved her, and who gave so much to the world and had so much more to give should no longer be with us. But her wondrous example will always inspire us and we will always be blessed by the warmth of her love.

Cows at Clandeboye, 2015.

LIVING IN THE MOMENT

Lindy Dufferin

This is an essay Lindy wrote for the 2005 book Late Youth: An Anthology Celebrating the Joys of Being Over Fifty, *edited by Susanna Johnston.*

Enthusiasm. That's the trick of staying youthful, flexible, curious and bendable. To achieve this, you are forever told, "It's all in the mind."

What a truism – but how does one keep the mind from dwelling darkly on unpalatable thoughts of growing old, decrepit and worn out?

Well, be enthusiastic. Even getting old and dying can be fascinating and, if you're lucky and live to a fine old age, it really can happen. I mean, you die – unlike the failed teenage dreams of becoming a famous and sexy movie star or winning Wimbledon.

Well... Armed with enthusiasm, you can use old age to do things that youth hates – such as giving time to things that do not necessarily get you anywhere. What follows are all sorts of surprises and delights of which you had no notion until the years pressed you into the unimaginable... Like writing this piece.

I'm trying to learn how to do things for pure enjoyment. In my youth, I was competitive. I remember making my pony miserable, being overwhelmed by a desire to win a potato race. Now I realise that winning did not matter a jot. What mattered was a happy pony and a happy me. I had no luck when I pulled, tagged and gnashed teeth. Now I go slow – love the pricked ears and sensations – with no bother about the result.

Every day has become precious. It was not so when I was a teenager. There were long, tedious periods when I did what I did not want to do, not knowing what I *did* want to do. Agonising self-doubt and silly vanities. Endless passions that blew me like deckchairs in a storm – hopelessly vulnerable – taking up airs and graces because I wanted to make an effort; to impress; to be attractive.

Thank goodness most of that idiotic behaviour has gone and now I can be what I want to be, paint pictures with love, enthusiasm and care with a Buddhist acceptance of the result: pleased and thankful if the outside world likes them but equally thankful if that is not the case – as long as I'm getting the awareness and pleasure of painting them and a calm acceptance for what it is.

I love my spaniel. He is now ninety-five and will soon be a hundred in doggy years. I am fascinated by how he deals with old age. Rabbits and rushing about have passed him by. Now he takes long rests, enjoys the fuss and bother that he causes, likes to be taken out in the car to look at the landscape, is very cheerful and makes the best of everything.

It seems that animals have learnt the art of living in the moment to perfection. They concentrate with all their being on doing what they are doing.

For the last month, I've been observing cows because I've been painting and drawing them. They, like my spaniel, have a busy and contented day. At no moment do they look out of rhythm with themselves or try to live in the past or the future. I'm not suggesting that we chew cud or wag tails — but there is a lesson there to learn: whenever possible, live in the moment with concentration and enthusiasm.

Now that I'm older, I do not have to be competitive or to achieve things: except to achieve things such as delving deeper into painting, loving others and making Clandeboye, my beautiful Irish estate, ever more a source of well-being for people to live in the moment.

So hurrah to old age — it offers such possibilities.

You have to turn it into a friend.

"Look here, old age, now that you've come to stay with me, tell me about all those miserable thoughts that people have about you. All that doom and gloom."

"I don't think you are right about that," says old age. "Can't you see that the past was full of youthful confusion? Heaven in a way, but all to do with getting enough, doing enough, achieving enough? Now that I've arrived and plan to stay, see the merits of life for what it is, and if you are an old human — keep wagging whenever you can and chewing over things with whatever mental faculty that still works.

"You'll be amazed at what happens, not only to you but also to your friends, both young and old. They love a dotty, ancient, enthusiastic relic. It gives them something to aim at."

Lindy's London studio after her death, with
her favourite beer.

ACKNOWLEDGEMENTS

Lindy had a fugitive soul – hard to nail down in a book like this.

As her friend Tristram Powell said of her, "My father [the novelist Anthony Powell] always said fiction was the best way of capturing the complications of character and circumstance, superior to memoir and biography."

Someone really should write a novel about Lindy one day.

But memories of Lindy are so vivid and unusual that they remain strong and fresh in so many of her friends' and colleagues' minds. I'm so grateful to the dozens of people who contributed memories of Lindy for this book. I'm sorry that not all of those tributes could be included in full. The number of letters showed a deep love of and respect for Lindy, spreading from Clandeboye to Northern Ireland, London and the far corners of the world. There sadly wasn't room to include them all.

Professor Jane Ohlmeyer of Trinity College Dublin was extremely kind in collecting memories from the undergraduates, graduates and academics who enjoyed four reading parties at Clandeboye.

They include Patrick Prendergast, Provost of Trinity College Dublin (TCD); Ben Kiernan, Professor of History at Yale; Jane Maxwell, archivist and graduate student, TCD; Elspeth Payne, graduate student, TCD; Dr Karie Schultz, graduate student at Queen's University Belfast; Rosie Lavan, Professor of English,

TCD; Dr Isabella Jackson, Professor of History, TCD; Yvonne Buckley, Professor of Zoology, TCD; Pádraic Whyte, Professor of English, TCD; Brian McGing, Regius Professor of Greek, TCD; John Horne, Professor of History, TCD; David Dickson, Professor of History, TCD; Professor Dr Iggy McGovern, poet, physicist and Pro-Chancellor, TCD; Professor Eve Patten, director of the Trinity Long Room Hub; Gail McConnell, Professor of English at Queen's University Belfast; Eva Muhlhause and Francesca O'Rafferty, administrators at Trinity Long Room Hub; Sinead Pentony, fund-raiser, TCD; Jane Stout, the "bee lady" and Professor of Zoology, TCD; Daryl Hendley Rooney, graduate student, TCD.

Deepest thanks to Tom Hayes and Carmel O'Sullivan, Professor of Education, TCD, who had a mass said for the repose of Lindy's soul in Dublin. Tom Hayes kindly reported, "We are getting a mass said for her. I don't know if she was religious, but it won't hurt!"

Very many thanks to the late Susanna Johnston for permission to use Lindy's chapter in her book *Late Youth: An Anthology Celebrating the Joys of Being Over Fifty*.

The following people have been most helpful and moving in their memories. Please forgive any omissions.

Kerry Adamson, Lola Armstrong, Christopher Balfour, Lady Perdita Blackwood, Bryan Boggs, Lizzie Buick, the Countess of Caledon, Charles Cator, Alice Cockerell, Walter Corr, Barry Douglas, Lord Dunleath, Nicky Dunne, Georgie and Honor Fanshawe, Michelle Farmer of Clandeboye Nature Rangers, Catherine FitzGerald, Arlene Foster, Professor Roy Foster, Lady Antonia

Fraser, Dr Andrew Gailey, Anamaria Gama and Miguel Nunes and their dear daughter, Carolina, Lady Getty, Catherine Goodman, Elaine Graham, Chloe Guinness, Sheridan Guinness, William Guinness, Tom Hallifax, Judy Hancock from the Royal Botanic Gardens Kew, School of Horticulture, Linda Heathcoat-Amory, Karen Kane, Fiona King, Lady Anne Lambton, Graham Little, Mark Logan, Elisabeth Luard, Rupert Lycett Green and the John Betjeman estate for their generous permission to quote from his poems, Peter Mandelson, Lucy McLaren, Bill and Daphne Montgomery, Brian Moorhead, Thierry Morel, Sir Van Morrison, Ferdinand Mount, my dear Dad, Robert O'Byrne, Michael Pakenham, Thomas Pakenham, Miranda Payne, Tristram Powell, Julian and Bojana Reilly, the Countess of Rosse, Willa Rumberg, Francis Russell, Rupert Sheldrake, Jackie Shields, Tom and Sabrina Stoppard, Gerry Summers, Lady Emma Tennant, Fergus Thompson, John Witchell.

I am so extremely grateful to my fellow trustees of Lindy's estate, Ian Huddleston and Dora Loewenstein, for their affection, kindness and generosity of spirit.

I am particularly grateful that they have let me quote from Lindy's diaries. The diaries have been so useful for finding out what she really thought. As she wrote in them in 2019, "The diaries are important for the future of Clandeboye – in truth, I had not realised this – very wonderful."

Many thanks to Richard Davenport-Hines for his early support for this book.

My thanks to Andrew M. Brown, editor of the *Daily Telegraph* obituaries page, and the *Daily Telegraph* for permission to reprint Lindy's obituary. My thanks to *Country Life* for permission to print the Girls in Pearls picture of Lindy. My thanks, too, to Ben Lowry, editor of the *Belfast News Letter*, and the *Art Newspaper* for permission to adapt my tributes to Lindy.

Deepest thanks for their lovely photographs to: the Earl of Antrim, Earl of Caledon, the Marquess of Cholmondeley, Walter Corr, Ana Gama, John Kasmin, Ömer Koç, Mark Logan, Thomas Pakenham, Christopher Sykes and Emily Ward. David Hockney was immensely generous in both the use of his paintings and in his memories of Lindy.

Sam Carter has been a joy to work with, full of cheery enthusiasm and planet-brained ideas. All thanks to Tandem Publishing, run by Sam and Alice Carter.

Lindy's great friend Sean Rafferty has been so thoughtful in the sad months since her death. His choice of music and musicians for her memorial services in Bangor Abbey and St Margaret's, Westminster, captured the deep sadness of her absence and the old joy of her presence.

Lindy would have been eighty in 2021, the year after she died. At the back of her 2019 diary, she had written the birthdays of twelve people she was characteristically going to give birthday parties for to chime with her 80th. I was among them. It would have been another act of great generosity to me – the latest in a long list of kindnesses that goes all the way back to my christening. Lindy laid down a dozen bottles of port from Berry Bros & Rudd, which I promptly downed on my 21st birthday.

In 2020, she was looking forward to the big day: "This

time next year, if I'm given the grace to be alive, I will be facing my 80th. The holy spirit, the guiding angels have showered gifts on me all my life. It has been an enchantment – a life of utter fascination. My passions have been intense and I've loved so much."

How sad she didn't make it. But she was philosophical about dying. In 2019, in her diary, she wrote, "I want an oak tree to be nourished by my remains or perhaps a yew tree."

At the end of 2019, she wrote in her diary:

> I will be buried with Sheridan in the Campo Santo [the family burial ground at Clandeboye]. Death. What do I feel? I think about it most days and see it as a beginning. Death always is the beginning – the order of life is such. The end of 2019 creates 2020, a new year. This last year has to pass. It would be total death – death to pass on to give space for new life.

Lindy often visited Sheridan's grave. In her diary for 4 February 2018, she wrote:

> The sun is coming up behind Sheridan's grave. To think he has been there since 1988 – cold but with the warmth of the spirit and protection of the earth and trees about him – to think that I might be fortunate enough to be with him in such a place. But till then I must do good things.

Oh, what good things you did, dearest Lindy.

Printed in Great Britain
by Amazon

37323026R00138